MARY TODAY

By the same author

CALLED
New Thinking on Christian Vocation

DAILY WE TOUCH HIM
Practical Religious Experiences

CENTERING PRAYER
Renewing an Ancient Christian Prayer Form

CENTERED LIVING
The Way of Centering Prayer

A PLACE APART
Monastic Prayer and Practice for Everyone

MONASTIC JOURNEY TO INDIA

THE EUCHARIST YESTERDAY AND TODAY

IN PETER'S FOOTSTEPS
Learning to Be a Disciple

JUBILEE
A Monk's Journal

O HOLY MOUNTAIN
Journal of a Retreat on Mount Athos

IN SEARCH OF TRUE WISDOM
Visits to Eastern Spiritual Fathers and Mothers

CHALLENGES IN PRAYER

MONASTERY

LAST OF THE FATHERS

BREAKING BREAD
The Table Talk of Jesus

MARY TODAY

The Challenging Woman

M. Basil Pennington, O.C.S.O.

DOUBLEDAY

NEW YORK   LONDON   TORONTO   SYDNEY   AUCKLAND

PUBLISHED BY DOUBLEDAY
a division of Bantam Doubleday Dell Publishing Group, Inc.
666 Fifth Avenue, New York, New York 10103

DOUBLEDAY and the portrayal of an anchor with a dolphin
are trademarks of Doubleday, a division of Bantam Doubleday
Dell Publishing Group, Inc.

Grateful acknowledgment is made to Costello Publishing Company
for permission to reprint "Our Lady" from their edition of *Vatican
Council II: The Conciliar and Post Conciliar Documents,* General Editor,
Austin Flannery, O.P. Copyright © 1975 by Harry J. Costello and Reverend
Austin Flannery, O.P.

Library of Congress Cataloging-in-Publication Data
Pennington, M. Basil.
Mary today.
1. Mary, Blessed Virgin, Saint. 1. Title.
BT602.P46 1987 232.91 86-29183
ISBN 0-385-23609-3

To
Mother Angela Norton, o.c.s.o.
Abbess
of
Mount St. Mary's Abbey
Wrentham
1952—1986
First American Cistercian abbess
a true spiritual mother

ACKNOWLEDGMENTS

First of all I want to acknowledge all those who over the course of the past two years have responded to my question: What would you want to find in a book about Mary? Their name is legion and their creative inspiration in shaping this little book has been totally pervasive. I want to acknowledge the members of my community who have said: "Go to it, Basil." Their support is absolutely essential. A special word of thanks to Brother Emmanuel and Brother Anthony for the drawings they contributed to this volume.

Above all and before all I acknowledge my total dependence on our God of infinite mercy, who has given me all that I am and have and has given it to me through Mary, his mother and mine. To her, for the grace and privilege of writing this book, I give thanks and all my love.

"He who teaches of me will have eternal life."

LET ME SING OF MARY

Let me sing of Mary,
Maiden, yet mother,
caring, ever present,
observing—the helping hand;
a mother, always here,
my mother, my cheer.

Let me sing of Mary,
God's own consort,
true queen of earth,
earth's gift to heaven;
the human close to God
to plead and intercede.

Let me sing of Mary,
ever appearing,
always one with us,
taking each our forms;
never foreign, always near,
a mother of tender mercy.

Let me sing of Mary,
a woman full and true,
the woman of my life,
so tender, yet so strong;
valiant woman ready to defend,
sweetest love of human's life.

Let me sing of Mary.

CONTENTS

ACKNOWLEDGMENTS   vii

LET ME SING OF MARY   viii

INTRODUCTION   xi

Mary of the Scriptures   1

Through the Centuries   26

Two Thousand Bishops   37

Mary Appearing   47

Further Reflections   66

The Woman   90

Our Response   98

Epilogue: The Challenging Woman   117

APPENDIXES: 123

    The Light of the Nations
        Chapter VIII: Our Lady
        —Second Vatican Council

    The Voice of the People of God
        Sensus Fidelium

INTRODUCTION

Who is Mary? The Mary we find portrayed in the Gospels and Acts? The Mary who is proclaimed to have been assumed body and soul into heaven? The Mary who has been appearing again and again in our world in so many different guises? Do dogmas like that of the assumption and the immaculate conception really change the way we know this woman? Who is Mary? And who is she in my life? Who ought she be in my life as a disciple, a follower, a friend and lover of Jesus Christ?

To these questions perhaps each one of us has to find her or his own answers. Some of us might prefer not to ask these questions, not to be bothered by them—at least not now. Others of us cannot escape them. Mary is not only "there"; she is *here* in our lives. We can't just ignore her. Somehow she has gotten into the fabric of our lives. After all, she is the mother—and a Jewish mother at that—of our Friend and Lord.

I was raised in what was probably a fairly typical middle-class catholic home of the pre–Vatican II era. Mother was second-generation Irish. Dad had Presbyterian upbringing. He had first come to know Mary as a young man at the peak of his romanticism. He probably got to know her more through his saintly mother-in-law than through the priest who instructed him in catholic beliefs. Among my earliest memories of church is fidgeting in the pew beside Grandma after mass while she prayed her beads.

I can remember October rosaries, the May shrines, the crowning of the statue of Mary, the processions of roses. The beads were in my father's hands when he died at thirty-three and while he lay in his coffin. I do not think I have ever seen a person die without the beads in her or his hands. They become a mute prayer when the lips can no longer manage words and the mind and heart are too weary to do aught but trust and want.

God has his own ways of reaching into our lives and touching our hearts. One day I picked up a little booklet from a stand near the door of our college reception hall and stuck it into my pocket. A few days later when I was riding a bus on Staten Island I pulled it out and began reading. That was January 27, 1951. That reading changed the course of my life. The booklet was Louis de Montfort's *Secret of Mary*. It argued for entrusting ourselves completely to Mary as Jesus had done in his conception, childhood and youth. Four days later I did that. In the language of de Montfort, I consecrated myself to Mary. Less than five months later I found myself in her monastery and I was given the name Mary. Five years later I would be consecrated a monk by the Church on the day honoring her birth.

Mary had loomed large in my life during my college days. As a young man thinking seriously of a celibate vocation she was very definitely the woman in my life. I was a very active member of the Legion of Mary. She received my flowers, my time and attention as we went about her Son's business. When I entered the monastery she still had a big place in my life, reinforced by the then prevailing practice of praying a daily office in her honor and of ending our day with the solemn chant *Salve, Regina* (Hail, Holy Queen).

But then Mary began to fade into the background. Her Son, the common center of both our lives, began to lead me to the Father. The communion in the Holy Spirit grew. I was led more and more into the simplicity of the Trinity. God was all.

At times, as I continued to take part in the marian devotions of my monastic community, the question would surface for me: Where is Mary in my life?

In the early sixties I found myself in Rome on the fringes of the great council. Mary was there—as a sign of contradiction. I remember Cardinal Carberry. He would stop each day after the morning session to buy a flower to place before the statue of Mary in his hotel room. Another bishop lamented that some of his fellow hierarchs "sat on their hands" when others were applauding Mary, in the course of the controversy. The vote on the inclusion of a chapter on Mary in the Constitution on the Church was one of the closest votes in the whole of the council, if not the closest. Mary's place in the Church and therefore in the life of each member of the Church was viewed very differently by different fathers of the council.

There is a great richness in the teaching of the Second Vatican Council on Mary—we will look at it—but in the end I came away with more questions. But the questions now rested in the context of a deeper, more settled faith.

I have let these questions be. And others have been added to them as I have been sensitized by the feminist movement, awakened by the base communities of Latin America and our bishops' pastoral on peace, visited Lourdes and Fátima and listened to the message of Medjugorje.

Who is this woman, Mary? What am I to make of her apparitions? What is her place in my life as a Christian of the late twentieth century, as a disciple and lover of Christ Jesus? How am I to express this? These are the questions I am seeking to answer in this book. The answer is not final. Nor is there an end to questioning. I want to live in the question. Answers tend to close things off. Questions invite wonder, growth and life. I am still growing and I want to keep right on. My relationships are growing—my relationship with Christ my Lord, and with his mother. May the reflections and partial answers found here foster continuing growth.

I write from a Christian perspective—catholic, if you will—provided you understand "catholic" properly. "Catholic" means universal. My concern is with Mary as the universal woman, the woman who has a significance for all women—and men, for the universe. Catholic names a special church among the churches with its particular living tradition and its particular gift to bring to the other churches as we come together to find fullness and strength in a renewal of Christian unity and a solidarity with the whole human family. As I write I seek to bring forth this gift, as gift, for all. I sense a special loyalty and responsibility toward the Christian community within which I find myself by the dispositions of Divine Providence. I want to help the catholic community to possess more fully its particular marian heritage so that we can make a fuller contribution to the whole Christian community and to the world.

Mary is very much the common heritage of all Christians. Her place in the life of the Christian community is already found in the Scriptures. It is a part of the heritage many noncatholic Christians are seeking to reclaim in a way wholly concordant with their commitment to Christ, her Son, our Lord, and with the Revelation he has left us in the Scriptures within the Christian community.

Lutherans know that Martin Luther was devoted to Mary, preaching, near the end of his life, one of his most beautiful and eloquent sermons on Mary's *Magnificat.* Calvin always saw Mary as the ever-virgin, totally responsive to God. The early reformers, in looking to the Fathers of the Church, found Mary and the Church closely linked in the patristic thinking.

As a man I realize a distinct disadvantage in attempting to write about Mary, a woman. Looking from the "outside" I will have a perspective, a sense and experience that comes from the complementarity of our sexes, but how much I do not have from not knowing from within the feminine reality! Thus this book is, indeed, partial, greatly needing the complementarity that a woman of faith can bring. I have tried to supplement for this by listening, as best I could, to many women both in person and in their writings. I am grateful for all that I learned as I prepared and wrote this, realizing better all that I have yet to learn and realizing more deeply than before the price at which celibacy for the freedom of the Kingdom is purchased. Foolish indeed is the married man who does not open himself completely to being enriched, deepened and sensitized by the woman at his side. He certainly has—to speak of only one aspect, the one relative to this book—a blessed opportunity to get to know and understand Mary through his wife.

Mary is one with us. We all form one People of God. We are all disciples of Jesus, saved by his redeeming grace. We each have our particular role among Jesus' people. What is Mary's particular role? It is important for us to know, for we are one people, one body. As we fulfill our own particular role, we affect the life of the whole and of each other. Mary's life, a life that in a very special way has been set forth as a life that goes on, can and should profoundly affect the life of every one of us. It can make a great contribution to our lives by the way it models and sources what is most important for us—our life in Christ, our life of faith and love, a love that mothers us and says a complete "yes" to God.

Mary's role exemplifies the ultimate role of woman—really of all of us, as she is the ultimate of all human persons. But she is a woman. As the feminist movement challenges the Christian woman and man to discern the feminine in God and the feminine's place in the plan of God, we can look to this woman who is first among women and expect to get some significant insights.

This volume makes no pretense at being an exhaustive, nor even a wholly coherent treatise on Mary. Dionysios the Pseudo-Areopagite, in his little treatise on mystical theology, which has shaped all subsequent thinking on the matter in the West, tells us that there are three kinds of contemplation. There is the direct contemplation which plunges right into the Divine and is wholly lost. There is an oblique contemplation which comes to the Divine through his creation, discovering more and more. And finally there is a circular contemplation, which, as it were, circles around the mysteries of God, penetrating more and more facets, letting the mysteries take more and more hold of us, forming and shaping us. I hope that much of what I offer here has been truly deepened and enlivened by direct contemplation. But what is actually experienced in such contemplation cannot be expressed in words. There will be many oblique rays. But mostly, we will be circling around God's greatest wonder in all our creation, apart from his own most sacred humanity, and seek to let the light of that revelation pour into our own lives that we may be more and more informed by it.

My writings come out of my life. Recently I wrote a book on my friend Thomas Merton. I wanted to take some time to get more in touch with him. This book comes out of my desire to be more in touch with Mary, with who she is in my life. I did want to get updated in marian theology, to share in what other women and men of faith are thinking and experiencing today, to understand more deeply the significance of Mary's current apparitions at Medjugorje. But for me it is never solely a question of the head, but always more of the heart, of life and living. I hope all that is shared in this volume is solidly grounded in tradition and modern Scripture studies and theology. That has been my intent and effort. But it is shared in the context of a lived experience. I want it to speak to your heart as well as your head. I pray that it might become for you, too, a living experience.

There have been some exaggerations in marian theology and more in marian piety in recent times. We should not be surprised at this. Such exaggeration is typical of love. Where the mind leaves off the heart goes on, says St. Thomas Aquinas. They will know we are his disciples by our love. Yet we do want to keep things properly focused, properly centered. As one moves through France, that first daughter of the Church, we are struck as we see in one city after another the magnificent cathedrals. Works of wonder, done at a time when there was so much less with which to work, they were the labors of love of the whole city's population. Almost invariably they

received a marian name and title, often just Notre Dame. And yet
Mary's ancillary role is so evident. She may have a chapel, usually
behind the main altar, a window, or be enthroned over the portal.
But the focus is always the altar and the cross. These are central, in
Mary's cathedrals and in Mary's life, and in the life of anyone truly
devoted to the Virgin.

As I was preparing to write this book, I asked many what they
would like to find in a book about Mary. A very common response
was to please show Mary as a very human and ordinary woman.
There is obviously some danger here. We could fail as much as
another age which wanted to exalt her as much as possible: *De Maria
numquam satis!* (Concerning Mary we can never say too much!). "Our
tainted nature's solitary boast."

We stand in danger of putting people in boxes which we have
previously constructed. I can remember taking part in an advisory
board meeting for an important movement. At the end of the meeting the sole black man got up. He vented a great deal of anger at
being treated, so he felt, as the token black. As he lashed out, a
paraplegic rolled up to the front of the room and responded: Blackness is not the only thing that puts you in a box. I stood up. I had on
my roman collar. And I added my two cents: Yes, blackness is not the
only thing. A spark of insight came into the black man's eyes. "Yes,"
he said, "as soon as you walked into the room I had you in a box." (I
am happy to report that we have become good friends.) We all tend
to create the space within which we receive others. To quote from
Aquinas the only bit of Latin I remember from his monumental
Summa, Quidquid recipitur per modum recipientis recipitur—Whatever is
received is received according to the mode of the receiver.

We United States Americans are very much equalizers. We have
to be careful that we are not just trying to bring Mary down to our
own level, so to speak. However, this widespread desire to see Mary
as one of us may not just be a question of our egalitarian culture. It
may, indeed, be the *sensus fidelium*—the unerring sense of the faithful, grounded in a received revelation and a living tradition and
guided by the "signs of the times," an invitation to come to a clearer
understanding of a facet of Mary that has only now been fully appreciated because her preeminent dignity and exalted blessedness have
been securely established.

Through history the faithful have struggled to understand and
bring into balance, harmony and integration the divine and human

dimensions of Mary's Son. Repeatedly, there was an overemphasis on one side or the other. Or, more commonly, one area of the vast Christian community was seeing more clearly one aspect, while another saw the opposite or complementary aspect: Alexandria and Antioch, Rome and Constantinople, Canterbury and Geneva. Christ shone forth in the many rays of his divinized humanity and incarnate divinity—too much for our faltering minds to take in and hold in unity and harmony. And so, understanding of the Mediator, who came to bring heaven and earth, the human and the divine back together, became a source of disunity, dividing us here on earth and leading us to act in ways that make us unworthy of heaven.

In this, as in all else, Mary has been like her Son. We have difficulty in bringing into harmony, balance and integration the facets of this, God's greatest creature, the human person most like unto himself, the Father's first daughter, the Son's mother and the most worthy temple of the Holy Spirit. Our diverse understandings of her still painfully divide the disciples of her Son.

Within the catholic community, we are emerging from a period which sought to do all it could to emphasize the transcendent greatness of this peerless woman. Today, as women emerge and seek to discern and find recognition of their true dignity and equality, there is ambiguity as to how to hold this woman. There is a sense that in exalting her, a male-dominated Church puts all her sisters down, regarding them as something less. Yet there is a suspicion and more than a suspicion, a sense, that a clear perception of the full integral dignity and beauty of Joseph's wife, a virgin yet a mother, a courageous widow, a woman of her people and a first among the disciples —that a clear perception of all that Mary is will do more for the advancement of feminine equality than any other claim or crusade.

As we dare to face the question Who is Mary? a realization begins to seep into our consciousness: As we open to the answer of this question we are going to have to adapt our whole perspective on the human reality, let go of some very deep-seated prejudices in regard to both women and men and accept ourselves and our sisters and brothers with a new challenging identity and relationships. Understanding Mary more fully and integrally can call us to new understanding of what it means to be a human person in this actual plan of creation where Mary's Son is the Redeemer. He is the head of a new creation in which where sin abounded grace abounded still more, in which the sin of sexual discrimination abounded and in which the grace of Christ called us into a oneness and a common participation in the transcendent dignity of divinity so that there is neither male nor female but only one Christ.

This is the challenge of Mary. For what is to be in all of us, already is in her. This is the meaning of the mysterious "assumption" of the woman from Nazareth. The most ordinary of human persons, one at the very bottom, the poor widowed woman of a subjugated and oppressed people, is lifted up beyond all the greatest and holiest, beyond what we can comprehend, because he who is mighty has done great things for her. And his very same mercy is active and effective from generation unto generation in the person of each one who reverences that mighty one with the "fearful" reverence due an almighty Parent-God and Lover-Friend.

To understand Mary better is to understand ourselves and each other better, to understand what it means to be woman and to be man, to be human and to be divinized, to be a pilgrim on this earth and a predestined heir of a heavenly throne. If we can begin to perceive something of the staggering, stupefying reality of this Nazareth housewife and mother, we can perhaps begin to get more in touch with the staggering, stupefying reality of our very own selves. In such a light, how can there ever be any prejudice or discrimination? How can there ever be anything but a profound fearful reverence for each and every human person, a reverence that rejoices in our rich differences, including that of sex, yet marvels more at our unique oneness in the reality of Christ.

It is, in some ways, an angry time in the Church. Perhaps it might be characterized as an adolescent period when many sense a need to break away from Mother Church to find their own true self in Christ, to become mature Christians who are able to love and care maturely. Part of the process of becoming an adult involves coming to care for our parents and take responsibility for them. The call of the Second Vatican Council—so different from the First—was for bishops to become aware of their collegiality and coresponsibility and for all the faithful to become aware not only of the universal call to holiness but also of their being the People of God with rights as well as responsibilities. We are a People whose strength and beauty, the fulfillment of whose destiny, depends on each member being fully who she or he is in her or his diversified reality. Children of innumerable nations, tribes and ethnic groups, inheriting and creating cultures, we are to bring all to the mosaic of the Church. In such an assemblage, leadership is essential, but it must be a leadership that calls forth and respects the full beauty and richness of each life within it. In such an assemblage an exalted queen held aloft, above and beyond the rest, is not so readily experienced as being one with us. Such a one is too easily ignored. It is the woman in the midst, as in the Cenacle on the day the Spirit gave breath and erupting life to the People, who is felt to be a part and significant. We want to see her in the fullness of her humanity and giftedness to be one with us as we strive to realize the fullness of our own humanity and to give expression to our own gifts to create a powerful, healing People that can reach out and bring together a fragmented and threatened human family.

The struggle toward self-identity, to find the true self, is today a longer and more difficult one. So much has fed into the construction and solidification of the false self, the fragile, defensive, competitive self that thinks it has to stand apart lest it disappear. There comes to my mind that day when Father Louis (Thomas Merton) stood on the corner of Fourth and Walnut (now Fourth and Mohammad Ali; Tom would love that change) in Louisville. He had built up a strong false image of himself as a monk who had to stand apart. It was a lonely place. But then suddenly, as he stood on that street corner, he saw the true nature of all the people passing along the sidewalks. He saw them all in their true beauty and being. As he perceived this true identity of the human person, he realized that he too was human, one with each and every one of these sisters and brothers. With all his heart he thanked God that he was just "like the rest of men." Interestingly, Merton saw this deep reality, this likeness, under the image of a woman.

In Mary we can find a woman who is truly one with us in all our humanity. Not all that special! Indeed, one of the marginalized, of an oppressed and often despised people, she was among the poorer of these people, at moments a displaced person, a fugitive and an exile through the machinations of oppression and bureaucracy. Always a woman—very second-class among men who pray each day: "I thank you, God, that I was not born a woman." I wonder if her Son had in mind this prayer, which he surely learned but probably never prayed, when he depicted the unjustified Pharisee: "I thank you, Lord, that I am not like the rest . . ."

Mary is one like us. And yet she is able to step forth in the midst of the most privileged of her theocratic people, the priestly ones, this hick from Nazareth in the sophisticated town of Ain Karem, and with incredible power and outrageous prophecy sing one of the most daring songs of liberation ever chanted by man or woman!

With such modeling as this in our midst and not enthroned in some ethereal realm far beyond us, we struggling adolescents can come to grasp our own true dignity, our true self in divinized reality, and then maturely take responsibility for "Mother Church" without being afraid of being smothered by her mothering or crushed by the inept exercises of authoritarianism within her hierarchies.

In this volume I am not going to attempt to develop all the psychological and archetypical dimensions of Mary as symbol. In part that would be beyond me; in part it brings us into realms replete with theories and hypotheses not always easy to reconcile and not always nourishing to our relationship with the person who takes on these symbolic meanings. While the symbol has reality, it has reality only in the minds and relations of real persons. I will touch on Mary's symbolic and archetypical role at times: the relationship of her symbolic role to the great archetype, the great mother, because there is much to be learned from this and our theology of Mary can be greatly enriched and brought into better balance by such consideration. But I think it is the role of the feminist theologians, before all others, to make this contribution. Like most men in the West, I am still struggling to integrate my own *anima.* As this integration develops I will be in a better state to enter into a living comprehension of the integration that exists in Mary, both the historical person and the symbolic reality.

We want the simple down-to-earth Mary because we want someone with whom we can relate, someone who can give meaning and hope to our very ordinary lives, in such danger of becoming hopeless. In the ancient hymn, *Salve, Regina* (Hail, Holy Queen), which we monks chant at the end of each day and with which the priest and the people used to conclude every mass, we declare Mary "our life, our sweetness and our hope." We know Jesus is the Way, the Truth and the Life. We want her to bring Jesus more and more into our lives, as she brought him to her cousin, so that we can be filled with joy and life can quicken in us. We need a little sweetness in our lives, the sweetness of being loved and cared for by an ever-present mother. And we need a source of hope.

The full weight of planetary culture comes upon us ever more graphically through the increasing impact of the media and the increasing interdependency we experience in sharing the limited resources of the earth upon which we have come to depend more and more. The needs from around the globe are staggering. How can an ordinary person hope to survive with his or her serenity intact, not to speak of "making a difference"? How can an ordinary, everyday life, such as most of us live, be at best anything more than a routine in which we immerse ourselves in the hope of being able to forget our meaninglessness? We look to this apparently very ordinary little woman from a very ordinary little town, the wife of a humble laborer, the mother of an only Child, and we realize that it was in living such an apparently ordinary life that she fulfilled one of the most significant vocations ever given to a human person, one that has made all the difference, that is the source of any ultimate hope that we have. It was in living such an ordinary life that she was prepared to do the one thing that ultimately matters for each one of us: she was prepared to offer with her Son the all-redeeming sacrifice of Calvary and thus merit entering into a full sharing in his resurrection and ascension. In her humble, hidden, quite ordinary life we find the hope that our humble, hidden, ordinary lives are making a difference, because we are living in accord with the mysterious dispensations of Providence for us. We are mothering the Christ in ourselves and in the world today. We are being prepared not only to offer the mass worthily each week or each day but to enter into the mystery of our own deaths, marked with the confident expectation of resurrection and eternal life with this woman and her Son.

Mary is, indeed, a challenge. She seems larger than life, more than woman, something divine, dare we say it? a goddess. And yet historically she was *just* a housewife and mother. What are we to make of this woman and all that men—and God—have made of her?

Every human relationship has infinite potential, for we humans are made for infinite knowledge and love. The excitement of a lifelong commitment to another, such as in marriage, lies in the commitment to openness and expectation. Each commits to being open to the other while the other commits to a loving exploration that will ever uncover more and more for both. The commitment I made to Mary in 1951 goes on. It has a lot more meaning and depth, excitement and perceived presence now. Mary is a woman worth getting to know. It is a privilege to have her as the woman in my life. My hope—and prayer—is that in sharing something of this exploration with you, Mary may become more fully a woman in your life, a challenging woman who will challenge you to be more of a person, a Christian, a disciple and lover of Jesus Christ.

September 8, 1986
Feast of the Nativity of the Blessed Virgin Mary
Thirtieth anniversary of my monastic consecration

MARY TODAY

Mary of the Scriptures

The Evangelists have written for us "the Good News about Jesus Christ," as Mark puts it in the first line of his Gospel—"accounts of the events that have taken place," to quote Luke. The Gospels are about Jesus, so we would not expect to find much about anyone else, though we would expect to find something about his family and in particular about his parents.

There is, in fact, quite a bit about Mary, his mother, if we listen attentively. Although, affected as we are by our modern approaches to such things, we are keenly aware that we lack many of the "essential" facts: When and where was she born? Who were her parents? When did she marry—and give birth to her Son? When and where did she die? Etc. Actually, we lack a good many of those facts about the main subject of the narrations. We don't want the fanciful details of the apocrypha but there is so much more we would like to know. We have, nonetheless, all that God wants us to have, and it is more than enough to get to know this woman and to develop a personal relationship with her. We need, following her example, to "ponder all these things in our hearts." Peter, whom Jesus constituted the leader of his apostolic preachers, the "rock" on which he built his Church, has assured us: "Everything that has been written, has been written for our instruction . . ."

We are speaking of a real, actually living Jewish woman. Christianity, like Judaism, is a faith whose point of departure is historical facts. Nonetheless we have to accept the fact that what has been handed down to us in the written Word is twice removed from the historical events. There were these realities, these historical events. Then there was the tradition, the handing on of the story within the Christian community. Only in time were men inspired by the Holy

Spirit and probably encouraged by the community to write down the stories, colored by the theological outlook of the community passing them along and by the evangelist himself.

The Gospels are primarily documents of faith, expressing the faith of a community, a true faith guaranteed by the Spirit of God. The Holy Spirit chose to give us these Evangelists' theological accounts of Jesus rather than eyewitness reports or verbatim records —which he could well have chosen to give us.

We have the Gospel of Jesus Christ, not the Gospel of Mary. This is the key to all right understanding, to gaining the proper perspective. Mary is to be seen only in the context of her Son Jesus.

Most of what has been written about Mary in the Scriptures in recent years has been written in the light of the historical-critical method. This method of investigating the texts does tend to call into question just about every statement found in the Scriptures about Mary. A clear bias almost always shows through in the writings of these critics. There seems to me to be a certain arrogance in interpreters who massively set aside the understanding and practice of millions of saints and sinners over many centuries. Was wisdom born with these moderns? There has been immense progress in some areas of biblical studies, but the fruits of this progress have to find their proper place within the whole of a living tradition and not seek simply to set it aside and supplant it.

We need to welcome critically what the historical-critical method has to offer. Without faith, a sense of tradition, the living presence of the Holy Spirit among the faithful, guiding within a community that has a divinely constituted teaching authority, and prayerful openness, we would have nothing positive to say about Mary, the mother of Jesus—only questions. But we approach the Scriptures with faith, guided by tradition, scholarship and a teaching authority and enter into a richness of life and love that is our proper heritage as a Christian people. The use of the historical-critical method for investigating Scripture makes very clear the inadequacy of seeking to base our faith knowledge on Scripture alone, not only in regard to Mary but also in regard to her Son.

Even if the stories we have been given under the Holy Spirit do not reveal to us the actual historical facts, they do convey the theological reality. They are revealed truth carefully written under divine inspiration. We are meant to draw from these stories the sources of our faith and hope and love.

Christian tradition has always recognized that the Sacred Texts have various senses, different levels of meaning. Here Scripture and Tradition flow together as the Fathers of the Church draw out, from beneath the literal sense, the spiritual and theological meaning. Such an approach to the Sacred Text is inspired by the Text itself. We find St. Paul, acting under the Holy Spirit, writing about another significant woman in the messianic line, the mother of it, Sarah, and her slave girl, Hagar: "The women stand for the two covenants." Paul sees these two individuals and their story standing for a collective people and their history. Mary, *the* daughter of Sarah, has a deeper theological meaning, like her forebear. Mary, like Sarah, would in herself bear but one child, but in bearing that one she would become the mother of a vast multitude. So the stories we find in the Gospels telling us about Mary do have a significance far beyond Mary herself.

Nonetheless we do not want to lose any precious glimpse of the historical Mary, the oriental Jewish woman, perhaps not more than fourteen or fifteen when she was explicitly called to the greatest vocation ever given to a human person. What she was called to was obviously beyond her comprehension. It still is. It is beyond the comprehension of any created being, even with extraordinary divine illumination. We are talking about God himself acting, bringing into being a God-man! That Mary was the recipient of some sort of special divine illumination is certain. She could not have fulfilled her vocation responsibly without it. This is the meaning of the angelic messenger.

* * *

Mary was one of a people very aware of their identity as a Chosen People, very aware of their history. Lineage was very important to them: they were the children of Abraham. Each person was conscious of being the descendant of a particular son of Jacob, a member of a tribe. They were a people of oral history as well as of the Book, or rather the Sacred Scrolls.

I recall a service in a very crowded synagogue on one of the high feasts. At one point in the festivities two of the distinguished elders processed among the congregation carrying the Scrolls. Everyone seemed to surge toward them, reaching out to touch, at least, if not to kiss their richly embroidered cover. This was a congregation of rather sophisticated and urbane Jews, yet here they were touching the heart of their faith. They were the children of the revelation, of the Sacred Word.

Mary certainly knew and loved the Sacred Scriptures. She knew and hoped in the promises. She knew her ancestry with its line back to David, to Abraham, to Adam.

It is curious how the Holy Spirit guided Matthew, the most Jewish of the four Evangelists, the one who saw Jesus in the context of the prophetic expectations of their People. As he traced the selective genealogy that led through the generations from Abraham, he included four women. Why these four?

Mary was certainly the daughter of Sarah of whom "the Lord took note," the mother of the race fathered by Abraham. Sarah was a woman of great faith, great dedication to the vocation shared with her husband, jealous of the destiny of her son. Her faith was sorely tested: the many, many years of sterility, then the heavenly annunciation. Did Sarah's experience come to Mary's mind when she was startled by a messenger from on high who told her of an "impossible" pregnancy? Did Mary, as she fled with her husband to Egypt, think of her mother Sarah making the same journey with all its peril? A child at her breast, Mary could not take refuge, like Sarah, in a ruse to protect her dear ones. She had to depend on the same Providence that ultimately protected Sarah. Again, as she searched for her lost Son did any thoughts come to Mary of that dread day when Sarah saw Abraham set off for Horeb with their young son? With Sarah did she wonder if he was lost to her forever?

As Mary faced the frightening demands of her special role in the history of her people she could draw courage from the example of Rebekah as well as of Sarah. Each of these great women was called, as Mary's Son would later call others, to leave mother and father, sisters and brothers and lands for his name's sake—to play their part in bringing that Son to earth by preparing a people, being part of his lineage. Mary could very fully resonate with the fearful concerns that Rebekah had for her chosen son Jacob as he followed upon his God-given way, facing the threatening jealousy of his own kindred.

Sarah and Rebekah lived a faith that kept them going through years of unknowing, a hope that endured the loss of all that was familiar, to respond to a call and a love that transformed their own will so that it was one with the Will of God.

But Mary's mothers, Sarah and Rebekah, are not named in Matthew's genealogy. Rather he names four foreign women: two Canaanites, a Moabite and a Hittite. What did Mary have in common with these? Why were they chosen to be listed? It is not easy to find a common denominator. Their inclusion could look to the universal call to salvation, the grafting on, as Paul would put it, of the wild olive, the inclusion of the gentile into the promised heritage of the Chosen People.

Perhaps, though, we are already seeing here something of God's option for the poor, or rather, the marginalized. Tamar and Bathsheba were exploited women. Albeit by a ruse she herself perpetrated, Tamar's father-in-law, who did not do her justice in her widowhood, used her as a prostitute. David's callous taking of the wife of one of his soldiers who was off fighting for him and then arranging for that soldier's death is well known. How strange it is that the most sacred lineage of the very Son of God should be passed down through such "scandalous" liaisons. God's ways are certainly not our ways—or rather, they are our ways. Our sinful ways he takes and makes his own life-giving mysteries.

Rahab, too, was an exploited woman, a harlot used by many men until God liberated her from her own people and brought her into the midst of his Chosen People.

Ruth's story is different: a beautiful story of self-sacrifice, faithful care and love aptly rewarded. Ruth accepted an early childless widowhood and yet remained a loving and giving person, concerned more about her widowed mother-in-law than about herself. God's ultimate care for her, giving her, beyond any expectation, the privilege of being in the messianic lineage, could have heartened Mary as she faced her own call—which meant in some way (the outcome was certainly not clear to her) losing her husband even before they came together—and hastened to the care of an elderly relative.

Perhaps there is no common denominator here save the unlikely choices of divine grace. No one is excluded from the divine call, from being included among the Chosen People, the family of God. The poor little girl from Nazareth could be and was the ultimate choice in the long line of promise, to be the actual mother of the one who was to sit on the throne of his father David. Perhaps Mary found it easier to believe and accept the astounding call because she was the lowly daughter not only of Sarah and Rebekah, but also of Tamar, Rahab, Ruth and Bathsheba.

* * *

No man can ever quite fully touch the experience of expectancy and creativity that is a mother's, especially during her first pregnancy. Every mother through the first months, although she is aware of changes going on in her body, has only a certain faith to tell her of the presence of new shared life within her. Mary's initial days of faith were even more special. The Life that lay hidden in her was a most special Life—the Source of all life. Though it is impossible for us to say how much Mary really understood, at the least she knew it was a boy and that he had a great mission ahead of him in life, that he was special, God's own Son. This could only have heightened the wondrous, growing excitement that is a mother's as the child in her womb becomes more and more an experienced reality, alive with promise.

One day a woman, undoubtedly a mother who knew the joy of bearing and nursing a child of promise, cried out in praise of Jesus: "Blessed is the womb that bore you and the breasts that nursed you!" Jesus took her immediately to a higher plane, wanting her to appreciate the thing he appreciated even more in his gratitude toward his mother: "Yes, and even more blessed are they who hear the Word of God and keep it."

In some way motherhood is relativized in the Gospels. We will hear Jesus even speak in oriental hyperbole of hating one's mother. For Mary though, things came together. It was in hearing the Word of God and accepting it that she became mother. For others of us, the hearing may call us to parenthood or it may not. The important thing is the hearing and keeping, obedience to the molding of God. Keeping the Word means free, active, ongoing consent as an open person. It means faith, receptivity, openness to God, responsiveness. It is a most positive and creative thing, something necessary for all men as well as women if we and the community of faith, the Church, which we form, are going to come to the fullness of our potential.

If there is an unbalance in our Church I think it is in good part due to the large-scale inability on the part of the male to be receptive. Too many men tend to see receptivity as a female quality. Men are to be formers, masters, initiators—this is the only kind of leadership that many men know; indeed, what they try to bring to relationships, to partnerships—with disastrous consequences. This is why the relationship and especially the sex in many marriages do not stay alive and vital: the male is not willing to open himself up and receive from the woman. Therefore he cannot be constantly called forth to ever fuller realization and expression of self in the relationship. He becomes locked in a deadly pattern and induces deadness in his partner. In lesser degrees this is true in so many other relationships between men and women within the Christian community and in the exercise of its life and ministry. From Mary we men need to learn how to listen and receive so that we can be creative—creative of Christ-life, divine life, in ourselves and in others.

Mary had been listening to the Word of God all her life and keeping it as best she could. This is how she was prepared to hear the Word when it came to her in an extraordinary way and made an extraordinary demand of her. She could comprehend something of what was being asked of her only because she had heard the Word of God, knew the sacred history of her People and believed and lived by the Promise. She knew that the Almighty could do great things for anyone who feared him from generation to generation.

Later the disciple whom Jesus loved would write; "To all who accepted him [the Word made flesh] he gave the power to become the children of God, to all who believed in him." Mary believed and accepted him and in becoming mother became even more the child of God. Mary is the first of the Christian faithful, the first to believe in Christ. In this she is the mother of our faith, a model of discipleship. For this is the essence of discipleship: to hear and keep the Word of the Master. At Cana she would tell us all: "Do whatever he tells you."

*　*　*

Already Mary had entered upon what was one of the more exciting times of life for any Jewish woman. She had been betrothed to a fine young carpenter. She still lived at home, but as she went about her chores she could pass by what would be her future home and perhaps see her man busy making it more ready for her coming. Her imagination could conjure up the happy day that was soon to come, the biggest day in the life of such a girl, the day when the whole village and friends from far and near would come to celebrate for days on end as Joseph took her into his home.

Then suddenly . . . An angel appeared, some way or another, and started to communicate with her. Angelic visits were not unknown to Mary. Since earliest childhood she had heard how angels came to Abraham and foretold Isaac's birth, a richly colorful story that tested the faith of an old woman and ended in the destruction of the cities of the plain. She would have remembered the other times when an angel came to her father Abraham, and the story of the angel coming to Gideon on the threshing floor. Angels were very definitely part of her history. But now here was an angel coming to her. Yes, she was afraid. What could it mean?

And then his message: She, Mary, was a highly favored one. She knew she was blessed in many ways, but what did this greeting mean: highly favored by God? The angel went on: she was to bear a son. She was to give the child his name: Jesus. He was to be great, Son of the Most High. He was to inherit the throne of his father David and rule—and rule forever. It was all too much, really. Mary was well aware of her Davidic ancestry. Yes, her child would be an heir of David. And obviously, her child would be in some way great; every mother's child is. Yes, a Son of the Most High, of course, all Jewish men are. But rule, and forever . . . There was a lot for Mary to question.

But Mary's question is not exactly what we would have expected: How can this be, for I do not know man. Mary was betrothed. The way in which she was to conceive a son would have seemed to be the least questionable thing about this annunciation. She and her husband would come together soon and just like any other couple they would express their love and rejoice in a child. This curious question has led Fathers of the Church to argue that Mary had obviously no intention of coming together with Joseph as an ordinary wife, that there was already some pact and commitment to virginity. Today's Scripture scholars argue that such a thing would have been impossible; it was too foreign to the prevailing mentality. We don't really know. What we do know is that at the moment the angel spoke to her, Mary was a virgin. And in response to her question the angelic messenger made it very clear that this special Child was not going to be the fruit of her and Joseph's love, at least not in the ordinary way. "The Holy Spirit will come upon you and the Most High will cover you with his shadow. And so the Child will be called holy and will be the Son of God." If the possibility of a woman committing herself to virginity was foreign to the mentality of the time, how much more so was this statement, if it was to be taken literally. Mary was to conceive a Child by God's immediate action. God was to be the father of this Child.

There are so many questions we would like to ask. What did all this mean to Mary? How much divine illumination did she receive at the moment to understand what was being asked of her? Did she have time to think of the possible consequences of this in regard to her plans with Joseph, in regard to the possible consequences before the harsh law of her people? There was a total openness and gift of self in Mary's response. "Be it done unto me according to your word." She was a complete yes to God. In that she accepted everything—certainly more than she could comprehend. There was a trust in God. That was ultimately enough.

In this Mary is so like us. There is so much we do not understand. The future has so many imponderables. As we seek and perceive God's will, we can only say yes, with confidence that he will be with us and it will all work out: for those who love God, all things work together unto good.

The angel was gone. And then it was pure faith. Did it really happen? Was she really pregnant? The angel had spoken of her cousin's being pregnant; was that a fact? Should she go to her? Somehow there was some sureness, the Spirit of God had come upon her, the Holy Spirit with his gifts of understanding, knowledge and wisdom. Through the mysterious workings of the Spirit Mary understood enough. Enough freely and knowingly to consent to her awesome role and to begin to take the steps that were necessary to fulfill it.

A divine delicacy gave her a sort of companion in all of this, another woman who was also challenged by an angelic announcement. Elizabeth's husband hadn't fared so well, priest though he was and the announcement right in the sanctuary of the Temple. But now Elizabeth was marveling in the experience of her announced pregnancy, one wholly outside the ordinary course of nature. Mary could find in her cousin a woman who could be with her with a deep empathy. How delicately caring is our God. How often do we not experience that he somehow manages to arrange that the right person is there when we most need someone.

As Mary made the long, unlikely journey across Samaria she had a lot to think about. There was all the wonder of the reality within her. A wholly new kind of communion between her and her God had begun. She had his Son within her. Perhaps she did not yet understand that he and the Father are one. But she did understand she was filled with God. Yet she was still the young maiden from Nazareth, only betrothed. What of Joseph? She left all that to God for the moment and went in quest of the companionship that the angel had indicated had been prepared for her.

We have always spoken of John as the forerunner of Christ. We usually think of that title more in relation to the role he will play later when Jesus is ready to begin his public ministry. But already here he is forerunner. When he leaps in his mother's womb he speaks powerfully to both of the mothers. Mary would not yet feel the Child in her womb but the prophetic Spirit in Elizabeth confirmed what she knew so vividly in her faith. There is so much of the human here in the meeting of these two cousins, and of the divine. From God's tender caring for Mary here, we can take some reassurance that he will care for us, even when we are in periods of confusion and uncertainty about our lives and what is really going on. Mary's way is the way to peace and fulfillment: a simple yes to God.

Mary, of course, could not have responded this way of herself. Nor can we. The Holy Spirit came upon her. In the power of the Spirit it is possible. According to the Gospels, the activity of the Spirit prior to the days of Easter was wholly directed to Christ. At the Last Supper he promised to send the Spirit upon his disciples only after he had gone. There is this one exception: the coming of the Spirit upon Mary, an essential part in the preparation for his coming. Mary was special and specially prepared, preserved from sin and specially enlightened by the Spirit so that she could fulfill in a fitting and proportionate manner her special role in relation to Christ. Gabriel saluted her as one full of grace, highly favored. The effect of her Son's redemptive mission was already at work in her even before he came, indeed, even from the first moment of her own existence. She was ever wholly God's. But in such a simple and natural way that not one of her relatives or neighbors seemed to be aware of her being that special. Even today many have difficulty in perceiving how special Mary is to God. There are always hidden saints in our midst.

After finding comfort and joy with Elizabeth, seeing her cousin's promised pregnancy come to a joyful birth, Mary returned home to find God taking care of Joseph, too. But there were some moments of pain and anguish for the two of them before the angel came to her husband. In the end, there was a deeper sharing and a deeper love as Joseph led his wife into his home.

*   *   *

In the meeting of the two women, Luke puts into Mary's mouth one of the great songs of history, a truly inspired piece. Here Mary is brought into an awesome part of her Jewish heritage, that of powerful women. She is one with Miriam, her namesake, the sister of Moses, and with Anna, the mother of the great prophet Samuel. Like Mary, these women of Jewish history were called upon to play an important role in subordination to a great prophetic leader. The earlier Miriam at one point forgot her subordinate role and sought to claim an equality that was not hers in God's design, and quickly enough she was put back in her place of dependence, needing the mediation of her brother. Our Mary rather celebrates her dependence: My soul magnifies the Lord and my spirit rejoices in God my savior, because he who is mighty has done great things for me—holy is his name.

Mary's role is in some ways more like that of Anna, a maternal role, and her canticle is also more like Anna's. But there is a deeper significance in Mary's likeness to Miriam. Moses was leading the people from slavery. There seemed to be no hope. Then they found freedom and victory by passing through the sea. This is what Miriam celebrates. Mary's Son is also liberator, the Legislator of the new covenant, who brings freedom to us all through the waters of baptism. This is what Mary of Nazareth celebrates.

Mary, then, rejoices not only in what God is doing for her but also in what he is doing for others, for all. In this prophetic moment, Mary's vision reached far: "all generations." And she saw them not only blessing her—Our Blessed Mother—but also being themselves raised up by God's redemptive work accomplished in the fulfillment of her Son's mission.

We might wonder how a very young woman, probably no more than fifteen, was aware of these social issues. How was she sensitized to them, living all her life in a small back-country village? I think we could almost say she lived in and belonged to a "base community." The men of her village would gather to talk, especially on the Sabbath, when they would visit each other's homes. The women would be on the fringes of the meetings, serving but not missing anything that was being said. Mary heard it all. From her study of the Scriptures she would have known much of the sufferings of her people, their ups and downs, of the power of God as a liberator. Now the men of her village would be talking about oppression: the oppression of the hated pagan Romans with their heavy taxes and their brutal executions. They would talk about hunger in the winter and the struggle to keep the village together, care for the orphans and widows and make ends meet.

In the base communities in Latin America today the *Magnificat* is sung with new meaning and vigor. In Mary's song, one finds the Gospel roots of liberation theology, a theology that comes from the heart of a faithful people, just as it poured forth from the heart of a young virgin: his mercy reaches from age to age to those who fear. He has shown might in his arm and he has scattered the proud in the conceit of their hearts. He has put down the mighty from their thrones and has exalted the humble. He has filled the hungry with good things and sent the rich away empty. This is the culmination of the old dispensation. This is the gateway to the new, the kingdom that belongs to the poor and the meek, those who weep and hunger. This is the Gospel of hope and ultimately of resurrection.

There is immense power in this song of Mary. In this it finds its heritage in the chants of the woman judge, Deborah, and in the valiant Judith as she brought back to her people the head of the conquering Holofernes. In the first prophetic reference to Mary in the inspired Scriptures she is spoken of as conqueror: she shall crush his [the evil serpent, the tempter's] head and he shall lie in wait for her heel. In the last prophetic utterance of the New Testament, in the Book of Revelations, the Woman will stand "terrible as an army in battle array."

These awesome symbolic images do not readily come together in our image of the humble housewife of Nazareth. But there was immense courage even in her hidden life. In saying yes to the angel and accepting her awesome mission, she was laying herself completely open to the unknown. She did not know what it might entail. It threatened all her plans with Joseph. It could even have meant being stoned to death as an adulteress or being hounded out of the community. There are hints that rumors hung around Mary all her life about her questionable pregnancy. In opening to the unknown, Mary's imagination might have given her some rather horrible scenarios. But was any one of them as horrible as the reality?

*   *   *

The birth of her Son was hard enough, in a strange town after a long, fearful journey, in an unsuitable cave or hut, intruded upon by nomadic shepherds. (Shepherds were a rather despised lot by common standards in Mary's contemporary culture.) She handled all of this, quietly pondering its meaning. Then, while the blush of maternal joy was still glowing on her cheek, just forty days after her Son's birth, in a most solemn and awesome scene, a terrifying prophecy was delivered to her.

Mary and Joseph had come into the great temple at Jerusalem. They came to fulfill the law. Mary, who had not known man, humbly submitted to the ritual. She knew that, in fact, she needed no purification. Did any woman really need to be "purified" for having given birth? Here Mary is in solidarity with all her sisters through the ages who have submitted to humiliating rituals that were administered by men who really did not understand what God intended and how he truly saw things. But Mary's mind was not dwelling on her humiliation but on the glory of bringing this Child into the house of his Father. What a new and different experience it must have been for Mary, coming into the temple that day, for she had a new relation with this awesome God of her people. She was the mother of his Son. There was an open and indescribable intimacy to which we are all being called because of the redeeming love of that Son. As Joseph offered the ransom of the poor for this Little One, the first steps were being taken to ransom us all.

For the happy young parents (if Mary can refer to Joseph as Jesus' father I think I can say parents) it was a moment of great pride and joy—which was suddenly, brutally shattered. Who would have thought the gentle old man who stepped forward and reached out to take the Child could be so brutal. Our loving Father sometimes seems so. There was a joy in the old man. His life's work was about to be completed. He had waited long for this moment, his great prophetic moment. But what did it do to the heart of the young mother whose whole being was centered in the bundle of love she had surrendered into his arms. "This child is destined for the fall and rise of many in Israel—a sign that will be rejected." And then he looked deeply into the eyes of Mary: "And your own soul a sword shall pierce." At that moment a shaft of pain tore through her. Her child was to be rejected!

By circumcision her Little One was brought into the covenant, by suffering and the shedding of his blood, largely symbolic, little, and yet real. And now by a further sacrifice, the dove of the poor, he was redeemed to find freedom and life among the people. It was apt that in the midst of living out these symbolic acts Mary should hear the prophecy of what had always been implicit in them through the many long centuries when countless numbers of other Jewish boys underwent these rites. The covenant of Abraham and all the rites and sacrifices that went with it pointed to the new covenant which was soon to be effected in the redeeming sacrifice of this Child in their arms.

Mary didn't know just what was the full meaning of Simeon's words. Perhaps she had some inkling it had to do with the suffering servant of Isaiah, but that would be the most she could have suspected. The old man had waited long to give his prophetic word. The widow at his side, who seemed to confirm it, had done the same. And now waiting marked Mary's life.

Indeed, waiting was always there. Like all her people, from the earliest age she was initiated into the expectations of a people looking for a Messiah. Then came the annunciation, and she waited like any other pregnant mother, only more so. Now another prophetic word was added to that of the angel Gabriel, and Mary waited with more dread in her expectation. She would, like any mother, wait as her Child grew up into his own manhood and destiny. She would wait at home as stories drifted back of his doings, of the mounting rejection. She was drawn more and more, by overzealous relatives, into the controversy that surrounded him, until that painful Passover, when all the city was astir about her Son. Then the dreaded news that brought her to his side and again a wait, three long hours on the hill while the life's blood she had first given him drained from his wounds and the life's breath he first gasped in Bethlehem escaped in a final cry. She went on waiting through that empty, empty Saturday until it dawned a new day and a new life dawned upon all the human family. Mary continued to wait quietly in the background as her Son completed his work and left for the heavenly home that was most rightly his. She waited prayerfully with the twelve and all the faithful for the coming of his promised Spirit. And then she went on waiting and praying as her Son's church, his mystical body, began to grow, she waited until the summons came: Come, my beloved, my cherished one, come. Finally her waiting was over. By a special privilege, in accord with the other graces she had already received and in accord with the extraordinary role her woman's body was called to play in the work of our redemption, she was exempted from having to wait for it. Her body would not have to wait in the tomb. Like the body to which she gave birth, her own would be borne into the heavenly places.

Certainly no one could deny the fittingness of Mary's corporeal assumption. But before the day of completed happiness would dawn, there would be many, many days of the greatest of sorrow.

It could not have been too long after the prophecy of Simeon had pierced her heart that an angel arrived again to shake up their life. By this time Mary and Joseph probably did not find the messenger so frightening, but his message was: to flee in the night. The powerful Herod with all his minions was out to kill, to murder her Child. Fear for the Child must have been so great that it eclipsed for the moment all consideration of the perils of exile. The pain of the route would grind these in once the Child seemed to be out of immediate danger.

How the sword must have turned in Mary's maternal heart when she heard of the atrocities at Bethlehem, of how the other mothers clutched their mutilated and murdered infants to their breasts still full of milk—because Mary had escaped with her Son. When I entered Mary's heart I began to understand for the first time why the Church has kept a day to be with the memory of this. The appellation "Feast of the Holy Innocents" somehow doesn't seem to be quite right. And I understood why we wore purple on this "feast"— the only feast of the year on which we did that. The change to blood red in the recent reform of the liturgical calendar is another sign of our need of the equal presence and voice of women in determining the way we live in our Church community.

Mary and Joseph with their Little One came into Egypt undocumented aliens, with all the insecurities that go with such a status. Joseph and Mary with their Little One were refugees from oppression—of course, if the "Immigration and Naturalization Service" of Egypt examined the matter they would have declared that there was no persecution going on in Palestine—who sought asylum and brought danger to those who harbored them, who gave Joseph some work to support his little family. Has anything changed? "Whatever you do for the least of my brethren you do for me." The María from Guatemala who "hides" with her husband and child in the sanctuary of the monastery, her mantle always shading most of her face, not from a religious sense or some modesty but to protect her very life, is the sister, the daughter, of Mary of Nazareth. Indeed, she is Mary of Nazareth today. Can any church, convent, monastery or school that claims to belong to Mary not open its doors to these sisters of Mary, to Mary herself, no matter what the governments have to say, no matter what the cost?

* * *

There would be many more journeys for Mary before that most painful one up Calvary's hill. There would be the journey back to her own country. It had its fears. What would they find there? They avoided Judea and headed for the more remote Galilee and the hill town of Nazareth. Perhaps they could find a quiet, hidden life there. There would be the pilgrimages to Jerusalem for the feasts. Perhaps Mary and Joseph were just beginning to feel safe on these journeys and had let down their guard a bit, when Mary shared with Joseph the harrowing experience of a lost child. How many, many parents know about this one. Three days and three endless nights. No wonder an anguished plaint escaped the lips of the woman who was used to pondering all these mysterious things quietly in her heart. You can sense in her words a special care because it was not only she who had suffered but also her beloved Joseph.

A mother's life is marked by the pain of separations: the initial separation as the child comes forth from the womb, followed by the weaning, when the child no longer depends on her for his sustenance; then the growing independence of adolescent years till finally the child leaves home to make it on his or her own. The fact of the matter is that all children at some point have to set off to be about their Father's business. The more parents can realize in faith that the Father does indeed love their children even more than they do, the more they can face these separations with peace and confidence. Unfortunately parents often see only peer pressure taking over and then children launching adult life so ill prepared for what the parental experience knows lies ahead. How much it will help faithful parents to get them through these difficult times if they can remember that their children are in some very real way Christ, the Child of the Father. Not only will such faith help the parents in their anguish, it will also help the children to recognize their Christ nature and dignity and to know that they are not going it alone, that they do have the Father's love and care—and Mary's.

Probably this is the greatest school of love for parents. It is a part of any love for another. We find ourselves so often powerless to do all that we want to do for the ones we love, to respond to many of their very genuine needs. We can only turn to the One who loves them even more than we do and who can take care of their needs. Such faith can preserve us from anxiety and fear. It is also important for our loved ones, especially for our children. Parents have the choice of instilling in their children the serenity and courage that comes from faith and trust in God or the obsessions of anxiety and fear which they experience when they do not trust.

Mary would have much cause for pain and anxiety as her Child went on about his Father's business. Only by choosing constantly to live the trust of her original fiat was she able to find the courage to stand by the cross and be one with her Son in the fulfillment of his Father's will.

*   *   *

As we come into the public life of our Lord there is evidently a shift in the relationship between Jesus and his mother, or at least in the expressions of that relationship. This is natural enough. It is also a cultural thing, and probably also expressive of theological reality. There are many variant interpretations of the scenes where mother and Son are featured together. The interpretations often show forth the prejudices of the interpreter.

We do need to remember the profound cultural differences we are up against: first-century oriental Jewish culture, filtered through Greco-Roman influences. It would be interesting to speculate: how different would have been the development of Christianity if the leaders of the new Church had turned to the East instead of to the West? Or if the Persians had extended their domination into Europe instead of the Europeans extending theirs into Asia. History is full of ifs. As people of faith we have to see the workings of Providence behind all of this. The way it has happened is the way that Providence allowed the revelation to be filtered down to us. We must be respectful of the course of history and humble in interpreting what is culturally conditioned.

The marian passages we come upon in the course of our Lord's public ministry do not seem essential to the Gospel or the Good News about Jesus Christ. Or are they? The inspiring Spirit and the early Christian community evidently thought they were to be included in the Christ story.

In part, the Jews needed to hear that flesh and blood was not the important thing. Rather, it was a question of faith and a response to life in the light of that faith: blessed are they who hear the Word of God and keep it. We, too, need to be reminded at times that it is not just a question of belonging, of baptism and Church membership. It is living faith and living the faith.

Mary's true greatness lies in that which is completely imitable, in hearing and keeping the Word of God. We, too, can bear and nurture Christ within ourselves, in a spiritual sense, in this way. It is important for each one of us to mother the Christ within. How do we do it? "Who is my mother, my sister, my brother? The one who hears the Word of God and keeps." We mother the Christ in us and in others in the same way Mary did, in the way she received the Word. When she heard the Word of God from the Angel, she responded with a total *fiat*—yes—and she lived that. Mary, in the exercise of what was her unique prerogative of being the mother of the Word in the flesh, was the first of disciples and the model for all who would be disciples of Christ.

We can understand Jesus' response to the woman who cried out: "Blessed is the womb that bore you and the breasts that nursed you," as a word in praise of Mary: "Yes, and more blessed is she who hears the Word of God and keeps." Some commentators rather see this as Jesus distancing himself from his mother. We need to remember that the Gospels as we have received them are carefully elaborated theological reflections on the story of Jesus. Luke took care to bring out right from the beginning of his Gospel that Mary did indeed hear the Word of God and keep it. Luke had Mary prophesy that "all generations will call me blessed." And here this unknown woman and Mary's own Son join to begin the chorus that will resound through the centuries.

Nonetheless there is undoubtedly some distancing taking place here. Humanly speaking, Mary, still a mother of flesh and blood, could sense this. Children do break away. All of us, and parents in their own special way, know the tugs of human affection that are left unrequited because the times and the seasons, duties and the evolution of life call loved ones on. Sometimes we do not quite understand what is going on. Sometimes it is the unrationality of the pain that makes it all the more painful. We want our loved one to go, parents want their children to leave the nest and go on to create their own life and destiny—but the pain of separation is there nonetheless. And there is not just the pain of separation but a sense of uselessness. We can no longer help, no longer be a part of the loved one's development and evolution. Our particular contribution is no longer needed—at least the one we have been giving up to now. If we fail to realize it is time for a new kind of participation and contribution, our pain will be all the greater. Mary had to search for the new role she was to play in her Son's life and mission. Her mothering of him according to the flesh was in a sense complete. Could a first-century Jewish woman hope to play a higher part than that of being mother of such a Son, one who taught with authority, dominated demons, healed the sick and raised the dead?

A new role was beginning to evolve. But in the meantime there was a lot of cause for fear and misapprehension. Mary saw her Son break out of the conventional accepted ways of acting, roaming about, making enemies, clashing with the accepted authorities. She even saw an attempt made in her own town to kill him. This was another effect of Jesus' option for the poor, identifying with them. The poor usually have little tolerance for one of their own who gets ahead. Mired in their own lot, they resent another who has the gifts and courage to pull himself out. Jesus accepted this with pain and sorrow. He rejoiced with Levi and his friends when they celebrated that one of their own had "made it," so to speak. Jesus would have liked to rejoice in the midst of his own in Nazareth, bringing healing, fuller life and hope to all his dear neighbors. But all he could do, respecting, as he always does, the freedom he has given us, was to pass through their midst, preventing them from further hurting themselves by hurting him. He got away safe that time. But that didn't end Mary's fears. She knew there would be other times and other places and he might not escape—would not escape. Was she beginning to understand the "Song of the Suffering Servant"?

How many parents today, relatives and friends and even children, can resonate with Mary's concern and pain here. Mary's whole training and way of life was marked by a profound respect for the religious leaders of her people. She trusted them and she totally trusted her Son. The conflict between them: how was she to understand it. Couldn't Jesus be perhaps a little more circumspect? Wasn't there some other way to say what he had to say and do what he had to do? Today's mothers and fathers, relatives and friends, brought up to respect Church and country, watch in pained silence or perhaps even loud lament as their young men and women protest war, apartheid and discrimination, batter nuclear silos and submarines, stand on the witness line in Nicaragua or witness in the slums of El

Salvador and the South Bronx, engage in life-threatening fasts and generally speak out and refuse to be coopted by institutional injustice and oppression. I do not personally know of any who have had to stand there and watch their son or daughter executed but I know more than one who have had their worst fears realized and with Mary buried a son or a daughter. And others who go regularly on visiting days to federal prisons, in some cases to receive the blessing of their priestly sons. And others who almost wish they could count on regular visits even in prison rather than live with the long absences and the constant fear, not knowing what dread news the next day may bring. May all these experience some consolation and strengthening in the knowledge that Mary is with them as a woman, a parent, who knows all the deepest feelings and anguish of their hearts because they have gripped her own heart. Certainly her heart is not less open, her compassion is not absent from those parents and loved ones who know a similar anguish as their young ones give themselves over to less noble but no less dangerous pursuits. The anguish here may not be so conflicting but it is none the less real and can be every bit as deep. The sorrowful mother is there with all the consolation compassion can bring. And always the ultimate hope that faith can bring.

However one might interpret Jesus' public stance toward his mother, we could never so vilify him as to think that he who made the first commandment in relation to our neighbor—honor thy father and mother—would not have honored his mother all the days of his life and into eternity. He severely rebuked the Pharisees who used religion as a pretext for not caring for their parents. See his compassion for the widow of Nain. He breaks all convention as a Jewish man and approaches an unknown woman. He even goes so far as to incur ritual uncleanness by touching the bier of a dead man, albeit one who will not be dead for very long. (The casuistical scribes must have had fun trying to figure this case out!) Could he have had any less compassion for his own widowed mother?

* * *

As we trace the relationship of Jesus and Mary during these public years two words stand out: woman and hour. They stand together in the first and last scenes where we find mother and Son together.

The *woman:* she stands mysterious and powerful from one end of the Scriptures to the other.

We find her in the opening pages of the human drama. Eve and Adam have betrayed a trust, rebelled, broken with God and allowed themselves to be dominated by the crafty serpent. But a compassionate and loving Creator, more mother than father, even as he metes out just punishment, promises help. A woman will come who will crush the head of the venomous serpent, even as he strikes out at her offspring.

Who is this woman?

Who did Jesus call "Woman"?

In the last pages of the revelation, there appears a mighty woman, "adorned with the sun, standing on the moon, and with the twelve stars on her head for a crown." She appears now with that offspring: "The woman brought forth a male child into the world, the son who was to rule all the nations with an iron scepter, and the child was taken straight up to God and to his throne."

Who was the woman to whom an angel prophesied that her son would reign forever, the Son of the Most High?

Modern Scripture scholars tend to see this woman as a collective: humanity or the Church. Before her, as the Book unfolds, lie the options: to become the red whore of Babylon who ultimately goes down into destruction, or to become the bride taken up into the nuptials of the Lamb.

What a twelfth-century Father has written, following the living tradition, I believe is true: What is said of the Church collectively can be said of Mary preeminently and of each soul individually. Each of us is to mother the Christ. Each of us is faced with a choice. Mary, preeminently. And preeminently did she choose to say her yes to the Lord, to be his mystical bride. Even as the Jews attributed the many beautiful bridal passages of the Old Testament to Israel, the Chosen People, Christians in their prayer and their exegesis have applied them to the Church as a people and preeminently to Mary. She is the woman who was at the side of Christ when upon the cross he gave mystical birth to his Church and assigned to her a mothering role: Woman, Mother, mystical Spouse.

Jesus spoke for the first time of his "hour" when he said to his mother at Cana: "My hour has not yet come."

Again and again as his mission unfolded he would speak of his "hour": "My hour has not yet come . . . I am not going up to the festival, for my hour is not yet at hand." In time it became evident what, indeed, was his hour: "Now the hour has come for the Son of

Man to be glorified. I tell you most solemnly, unless the grain of wheat falls on the ground and dies, it remains only a single grain; but if it dies, it yields a rich harvest." "Father, the hour has come: glorify your Son so that your Son may glorify you; and through the power over all that you have given him, let him give eternal life to all you have entrusted to him."

Perhaps one of the most troublesome koans of the New Testament, one of the most enigmatic questions of the Gospels is the one Jesus addresses to his mother at the first mention of his hour: "What is it to you and to me, Woman?"

It could be simply said that the use here of the title "woman" indicates the defining of a new relation between these two persons. The request, then, which might have been but a mother's request to her Son to help out in a particular domestic need, has to be seen in another context and have relevance to the "woman's" role in that context. What actually happens? Already this woman seems to know what Jesus will later state: Ask and you shall receive. With unhesitating faith she sets things in motion to enable her Son to give what she has requested. There is no hesitation on her part. She knows he will act and she instructs the others to be ready to do what he tells them. The result of her faith? Not just an abundant supply of first-class wine, the relief of the particular need the woman had set forth, but Jesus worked his first "sign" and his disciples believed in him. Mary, in her new role which was already present in her old and ever-present role, modeling faith, was mothering faith among her Son's disciples.

The shift had actually begun much earlier, or rather the first intimations of it come some eighteen years earlier in the story. Jesus' action on that occasion could be seen simply as a not untypical adolescent prank—if that word is not too irreverent. The Twelve-Year-Old's first trip to the big city. The curiosity, the wonder. He sought out his natural heroes, the wise men of the Temple who held everyone's awe and respect in this theocratic society. He listened rapt, and his own brightness shone forth in the sharpness of his questions. It was all very exciting, no thought for worried parents. And when they did arrive on the scene, a rather adolescent response: Why'd you worry? You should have known what I was up to. But there is obviously something more in this Adolescent's "prank." The hint of it in his response left a concerned mother even more concerned and wondering. She spoke of the man at her side as his father. Her context was the family of Nazareth: Jesus, Mary and Joseph. His response spoke of another Father, the context was a universal family.

What was to be Mary's role in this other family of her Son?

John seems to make it quite clear. He chooses the ultimate moment in the story of Jesus, the moment when Jesus mystically gave birth to this new "family." We listen to the last words of a great man with most special attention, words to be ever cherished. John here again puts into Jesus' mouth the title "Woman." And he surrounds it with five repetitions of the word "mother." It is most clear. Jesus' charge to the beloved disciple, the prototype of all disciples: "Behold your mother"—after saying to the woman, her role, her charge, clearly stated: "Woman, behold your son."

Mary's role as the *woman* is but an amplification of her native role of mother. Mother of the Christ, mother of his disciples, his friends, his beloved ones. What could be more natural for a Jewish mother! To her, every one of us is her only child.

Mary is the mother of disciples. She is the one who mothers faith in us by modeling for us what it means to hear the Word of God and keep it.

In regard to this I think it is good to note that the Scriptures do make it clear that a growth process did take place in Mary. She didn't always have it all together. Luke tells us explicitly that she at times did not understand what was going on in her life with God, she did not understand what her Son was about. She had to sit with questions and wait. She abided in openness and awaited God's time. She waited in the upper room with the twelve and all the other disciples for the coming of the Spirit who according to the promise of her Son would teach them all things, bringing to mind whatsoever he had said to them.

Luke tells us more than once that Mary "pondered all these things in her heart." I think this is an important statement. Quite evidently so did Luke, the community of faith from which he was drawing and the inspiring Spirit. It is repeated verbatim more than once—something very unusual in the Gospels. The text does not say, as one recent translation badly puts it: she thought all these things over. It is not a question here of thinking, of trying to master the realities of faith, the mysteries of life. Most of us men are all too prone to constantly approach things in this way. To try to dominate them and reduce them to something our poor little minds can possess. That is not the process here. It is rather a question of letting the realities of faith be with us, enter into us, and reveal themselves to us, a matter of letting ourselves be molded by them.

I think women tend to be better at this and seem to sense more clearly the need for it. Their lives seem to be much more communal, they are present and caring all the time. Thus they sense the need at times to let go and be with reality. We men tend to live more isolated lives psychologically. We tend to be more competitive. When we come together we tend to want something more active, interacting, a grappling with the matter at hand, be it liturgy, prayer group or Bible study. Here as elsewhere we can complement and help each other toward integration and fullness. We men need to learn to ponder in the heart, not just think in the head. Let the reality rest in us, lovingly held, ourselves laying open, willing to be transformed, receptive. In this sense we need to be "feminine," to allow our feminine side to be actively passive. Women need to help men to create communal worship that is less lacking in this element of receptiveness.

In this regard perhaps we need to add to the precept requiring us to come together weekly for worship, the precept, or better, an expectation, that each Christian each week will also take some quiet time to ponder in the heart, a weekly time of retreat, of contemplation. When I say weekly I am speaking in the context of our present ecclesial expectation. This is minimal. What is much to be desired is that the Eucharist would be for all a daily food; a daily coming together in some communal way to celebrate and hear the Word would be immensely empowering. At the same time, most lives would be vitally sourced by one or two periods of meditation each day. The coming together and the pondering can be one as families or friends support each other by sitting together in the silence.

Mary's tradition called for the morning and evening prayer when the heart opened to hear and receive again the *Shema Yisroel:* Hear, O Israel (the individual and the community blend into one), the Lord the God is your God, and there is no God but he. So that Israel might, hearing this Word, keep it forever.

The life of Mary of Nazareth, the life and mission of the mother of God and the mother of the faithful, was a life deeply involved in the human condition, in the details of human life. She grew up like any other child of her village. No one saw anything special in her. She was betrothed and dreamed of the marriage and married life. She was pregnant and knew that special intimacy of sharing this with another woman. She gave birth to a child, received guests, traveled. She went to services and celebrations, took care of her family and prayed with them. She had her worries, not the least of them her Child and his future. She watched by a dying loved one and laid him to rest. If she didn't know sin in herself, she knew it far more deeply than most of us in experiencing its consequences in her Son. Is there anything human, anything fundamental in our human lives, that did not touch this woman of Nazareth?

And there is nothing in the graces of Mary that is meant to be foreign to us either. What God did for her he wants to do for each one of us. He wants us all to be free from sin and all the bonding of sin by the grace of Christ Jesus. He wants us to be fully integral and alive. He wants to form his Son in us. He wants us to bring him to others for their joy and ours. He wants us to intercede effectively with unwavering faith, caring for the needs of others. He wants us to follow Jesus and share in his passion. He wants us to receive the Holy Spirit in the midst of the Church. He wants us to enter into the joys of heaven in the totality of our human existence, body as well as spirit.

In all, Mary is the first of the faithful, model of faith and faithfulness, mother of beloved disciples.

And now, enough said; it is time to ponder all these things in our hearts.

Through the Centuries

We were sitting in a circle, about a dozen of us. The brother who was leading the group had a sizable box on his lap. He gently lifted out of it a rather large ball of putty. The surface of the ball glistened, a shiny smooth surface. Brother held the ball for a minute or so, his hands firmly but gently embracing it; the loving care was very evident. He then with continued care handed the ball to his neighbor and invited each of us to take our turn with the ball. By the time it arrived back to Brother it was not significantly changed, but its previously shining surface was now almost totally marked by the imprints of our many hands. Some careful tracing could probably discern the different imprints.

This is tradition. The reality, whether a thing of revelation or a thing of history, is placed in our hands. And we pass it along, from generation to generation. Provided no one drops the ball or acts violently, the reality passes down the course of history without any essential change. Yet each recipient who has taken it into his or her life and has passed it on has left an imprint, for better or worse.

The imprint of a loving reverential heart is a beautiful thing. A mind that is set on mastery or determined to fit the tradition into some preconceived pattern is apt to do some violence to the essential shape of the tradition, mar or truncate it in some way. Undiscerning love in its subjectivity or emotionality can obscure the essential form it overlays. From time to time, someone who is certain in regard to the essential form needs to do some reshaping and cleaning up. Thus the tradition is passed on through its many vicissitudes.

The Christian religion is a way of faith whose point of departure is a collection of historical facts clustered around the one essential event: the incarnational redemptive mission of the Son of God. Close by the central figure, playing an essential role in his becoming man, is his mother. Mary stands in history.

A Jewish woman, she expresses a living tradition, which, through her, passes on to her Son and into the living tradition of the Church which he establishes. Holding that tradition in her heart and in her life, Mary made her own special, personal imprint on it as she passed it along. It was an imprint not out of harmony with all that went before; rather it brought all of that to an undreamed fullness. In doing that Mary herself became the source of a very rich tradition.

The *Mater Dolorosa*, the sorrowful Mother, is probably not the most popular image of Mary among Christians today. We have been turned off by too many oversentimental hymns—or perhaps just the sentimental way they are sung, for the *Stabat Mater* is of classical beauty—and pictures and statues that border on the grotesque. But that Mary was a woman who knew profound sorrow in her life is a solidly biblical concept. The *Mater Dolorosa* is not a theological concept but a real person who in the strength of her faith, hope and love was never defeated by her unspeakable sorrow. We do not want to forget that this woman walked this earth, heard Simeon's frightful prophecy and lived through its fulfillment.

For our Jewish brothers and sisters who have any sense of the Mary of Nazareth, this particular dimension of her reality is the one that strikes the deepest and most responsive chord. The tragedy of this Jewish woman is an aspect of the uninterrupted path of suffering along which her sisters have walked in the centuries before her and in the centuries after her. Mary is one with Rachel, Jacob-Israel's wife, mother of the Jewish people, who has had to bewail ceaselessly the sufferings of her children. Mary's Son, like many another Jew, was executed by an oppressor of the Jewish people. We Christians tend to forget that every Jewish martyr is bonded with Christ's death on the cross just as is every Christian martyr, albeit by a different bond. Mary standing at the cross is one with every Jewish woman as well as every Christian woman who has witnessed a loved one die because they belong to the People of God. Any kind of anti-Semitism is totally inappropriate for a people who take their name from the anointing of a Jewish Rabbi as Messiah of his people and who look to that Rabbi's mother as their mother and advocate. We do not want to lose sight of the universal human validity of Mary.

Through her sufferings, one with her Son's, all human suffering becomes a vehicle for holiness and new life.

Mary connects Jesus with the Jewish people, a living tradition. Mary lived, according to Luke, a life determined by the Jewish religious tradition. There is no indication that she was in any way critical of it even though it reduced women to such second-class status or lower. The Jewish woman was virtually a possession of the men in her family, like the animals of the farm. In the Jewish enumeration of the ten commandments, what we usually separate as nine and ten stand as one: You shall not covet your neighbor's wife or his servant, man or woman, or his ox or his donkey or anything like this. It was the later preoccupation of a celibate hierarchy that reorganized the ten, separating out the wife, giving a basis for all the moralizing on sexual thoughts and desires, something unknown in Jewish moral considerations and hardly to be found among the Orthodox Christians.

Mary lived and died a Jew. I do not think anyone could imagine her, great as was her sorrow and incalculable pain, ever speaking out in anger against the Jews, labeling them God-murderers. She knew that her Son died out of love and in love with his people.

Mary's name was Miriam, a name shared with many notable women in Jewish history from Miriam, the sister of Moses to Miriam, the wife of the cruel Herod who had her executed just as he had executed the little boys in Bethlehem. It was an exceptionally popular Jewish name at the time of Christ. We see how common it is among his disciples: Mary the penitent, Mary of Magdala, Mary of Bethany, Mary the wife of Clopas and the other Mary. Her name expresses Mary's connectedness with her people and her times.

I would note in passing, it is exceptional and significant that we know the names of so many of Jesus' women disciples. This is uncommon; women were not named. We are given the names of his brothers but not of his sisters. We don't hear the name of Peter's mother-in-law, not to speak of his wife. But Jesus' women disciples are named equally with the men. And this carries over unto Paul. And into the early Christian tradition where women stand side by side with men in the Church of the martyrs. What happened afterward to this respect Jesus and his first disciples showed for women?

Another facet of the Jewish tradition that throws light on Mary is the role of the queen-mother. We see this especially in the homage that Jesus' ancestor David paid to his chosen queen, the beautiful

Bathsheba. It was very much a part of the oriental tradition. If Christ was a king, and this he made very clear in his testimony before Pilate, where the whole conversation seems to circle around this divine-human kingship—so much so that Pilate insisted that this title be placed above Jesus on the cross—then who is his queen? That development of doctrine which came to see Mary as the queen mother, while it may be a bit foreign to the culture of some of us, was very natural to hers and that of her Son. The powerful advocacy of the queen mother, which was already hinted at at Cana, was something that the Christian community became very conscious of in succeeding centuries.

* * *

As Jesus stood atop Olivet, the city of Jerusalem stretching out on the other side of the valley, his chosen disciples clustered around him. They had enjoyed his presence little enough in the course of the past forty days. Now they sensed it was to be withdrawn from them altogether. Even as they talked to one another their eyes kept coming back to him, fixing on him, drinking in the vision. If there was no comeliness about him on that terrible Friday, now he was the most beautiful of the sons of men; each time they saw him he seemed more beautiful.

He gathered them about. It was the moment of the final charge: Go forth and teach all nations . . . Even as the clouds took him out of sight, their eyes were still drawn to him as though by some powerful magnet. It took angels to break the spell—Men of Galilee, why do you stand here looking up to heaven—and send them on their way. In an amazingly short time the Church embraced women and men of many nations. And the number has never ceased to grow. Each member has received the ball of tradition, has had the opportunity to hold it lovingly and make her or his impress and then pass it on. The ball has been passed around and back and forth across national and racial and cultural lines.

It is no wonder then that we have the phenomenon which we speak of as the "development of doctrine." The simple truths of the Revelation, deep with all the depth of the divinity, have been lovingly held and examined and expressed by the minds and hearts of hundreds of peoples and nations. Each has made her or his impress, each has been able to bring out another facet of the height and depth and length and breadth of the mysteries of the God-man.

In the midst of agonizing controversies, as fervent but fallible followers overemphasized one or another facet and dented and damaged the ball of tradition, the first councils sought constantly to bring things back into harmony. The depths set forth in simple Semitic similes were painstakingly translated into finely tuned Greco-Roman philosophical terms and concepts. It was the work of centuries. Greek words were created and consecrated, then the apt Latin translations. But every translation is a traitor. No more could the Latin capture the Greek than could the Greek capture the Aramaic or the Hebrew. As the mysteries of faith jumped the borders of nations and peoples, the struggle went on, as language after language sought to speak of a God-man, a "person" with two "natures," three "persons" with one "nature," "sacramental" presence and so on—words and concepts colored with connotations and historical footnotes. As points were argued with the fervor of the yeshiva, light burst forth again and again, and more and more of the beauty of the mystery was revealed. This was the development of doctrine taking place under the guidance of the Spirit who had been promised to teach us all things, bringing to mind whatsoever the Master had said to us. It is a process that is far from complete, even though hierarchs have again and again tried to get control of things by binding the living mysteries in static and therefore dead and deadening concepts.

Mary is certainly very much in the midst of this development of doctrine and doctrinal understanding. If anything the Gospels show this humble woman working her own way toward ever fuller understanding—she who is the perfect imaging of his Church. She didn't understand everything. She had to ponder in her heart. She dared to question even angels. She listened. She prayed. She waited. She had faith. And she found herself a part of the mystery that was unfolding.

Perhaps she never was as obtuse as those first twelve "bishops." They had first to learn to listen, and that was quite a process. They had the very best of teachers, and yet as the last lesson was drawing to a close, Jesus would lament: Have you been so long with me and you do not yet understand? He promised another teacher, one who would at moments come dramatically from without, but who would constantly work from within. These men would come to understand. And even more, they would learn how to make others understand, women and men so diverse as those of Madras and Rome, Macedonia and Mesopotamia. How different are the Jesus of Jerusalem, the Christ of Kerala and the Lord of the catacombs, yet they are the same.

When the bishops of many nations gathered at Nicaea in 325 and in Constantinople in 381 to hammer out that formula of faith which we still recite each Sunday in our Eucharistic gatherings, they were bringing to consummation an enormous development of doctrine that has given us a norm against which to measure in part all succeeding growths in doctrinal understanding. No legitimate development could ever go against what was set forth in those assemblies. The Lord had promised his guiding Spirit. He was there as he has been in every succeeding ecumenical council, helping the Fathers to strain out true development from false.

It was at the third of these councils, held at Ephesus in 431, that the development of doctrine concerning Mary was highlighted. It was postulated by the refinement that was coming out of the Christological controversies. It had become very clear that Mary is indeed the *theotokos*, the God-bearer. The Latins translated this into *mater Dei*, mother of God—not quite the same, and a translation which never pleased the Greeks.

Development continually opens up the way to new questions and further development. The creed elaborated by the first two ecumenical councils declared Jesus *natus ex Maria virgine*—born of the virgin Mary. Just what is the full implication of this? It has been disputed. Does this mean only that Mary had no sexual relations up to the time of Jesus' birth? Does it include the preservation of Mary's physical organs in a virginal state even in the birth? Does it include the belief that Mary was ever virgin in spite of her having a husband? Roman Catholics have believed all of this to be true though they have not necessarily believed that all of this is included in this particular statement of the Creed.

Solemn definition and development of doctrine have not always gone hand in hand. Doctrinal insights already proposed by Fathers of the Church sometimes took centuries to come to solemn formulation. St. Epiphanus wrote in the fifth century, "Mary by grace was free from all stain of sin." Such an affirmation includes the doctrine of the immaculate conception, which was solemnly promulgated only in 1854.

Parallel with the development of doctrine and intermingling with it was the development of popular piety, expressed in many ways,

The Keeper of the Portal, XII Century, Sinai

colored by many cultures. Compare the sobriety of the early Latin prayer *Sub Tuum* with the rich splendor of the most popular Greek prayer, the *Akathistos,* and the more emotional piety of the medieval Latin prayer of Bernard of Clairvaux, the *Memorare:*

Sub Tuum

We place ourselves in your keeping, holy Mother of God. Refuse not the prayer of your children in their distress, but deliver us from all danger, ever virgin, glorious and blessed.

Hymnos akathistos

Hail, Mother of the most holy Star;
Hail, Morning Light of the mystical Life.
Hail, you who extinguish smoldering error;
Hall, you who show their majesty to all
    consecrated to the Trinity.

Hail, you who drive away brutality and inhumanity;
Hail, in Christ we see the friend of humanity as Lord.
Hail, you who free us from pagan worship;
Hail, you who preserve us from the offspring of discord.

Hail, you who put an end to the worship of fire;
Hail, you who free those who are obsessed with greed.
Hail, you who show the faithful the path of Wisdom;
Hail, you who fill all creatures with bliss.

Hail, you virgin Mother.

Memorare

Remember, O most gracious Virgin Mary, that never was it known that anyone who fled to your protection, implored your help or sought your intercession was left unaided. Inspired with this confidence, I fly unto you, O Virgin of virgins, my Mother. To you I come, before you I stand, sinful and sorrowful. O Mother of the Word Incarnate, despise not my petitions, but in your mercy hear and answer me.

Marian art, too, reflects the times and cultures, something Mary herself legitimized when she gave to Juan Diego an image of herself as a young Aztec maiden, painted on a humble tilma. The simple frescoes of the catacombs put us in touch with the Jewish Mary, so plainly human. Icons—the oldest we have is from the fifth century, though some allegedly come from Luke the Evangelist—introduce the hieratic beauty of Byzantine splendor. Medieval stained glass moves again toward a later humanism, where Mary finds herself a medieval princess and the like. Today, she may appear with the gracious beauty of an African black or the delicate finesse of a Japanese.

We could go on and on. Popular piety flowed most strongly into the development of doctrine when it was as it were canonized by being incorporated into the official prayer of the Church, the liturgy. *Lex orandi, lex credendi*—the law for praying is the law for believing. We see this most strikingly in the solemn formulation, which took place only in 1950, of the doctrine of the corporeal assumption of the Blessed Virgin. In setting forth this doctrine Pope Pius XII appealed primarily to the age-old liturgical celebration of the feast. For many many centuries it had been the primary feast of Mary throughout Christendom. In the East it was preceded by a minor "lent." In the West it had not only its vigil and fast but also an octave, eight days of continuous celebration. The feast of the conception of Mary without sin was celebrated universally for several centuries before it received its doctrinal promulgation.

Jesus' full revelation has been absorbed only slowly and haltingly into the consciousness of the Christian community. There is evidence that something of what was present in the first communities of faith—a fullness of goodness that was too good, when the Church of the martyrs lost its radical fervor, a fervor that was so truly converted from the values of the transitory world that it was ready to let go of life itself—it lost, too, something of its grasp on the fullness of the Good News. It has only gradually reappropriated it.

An example of this would be the Eucharist. In the early Church all the faithful partook of communion at every liturgical celebration. The awesomeness and expectancy of this intimacy with the Divine was too much for any but the truly fervent to hold. In time it was lost as, more and more, the faithful held back. Only in our century did a saint, Pope Pius X, seek to renew the primitive consciousness. The Second Vatican Council in the renewal surrounding it, especially in its liturgical aspects, has been completing that saintly pontiff's work. We are again in an age of martyrs. Many are lamenting the increasing number of Christians who stray away from the faith. But a new fervor marks those who choose to stay and regular communion is their practice.

The development of doctrine is not always necessarily a progress. The ball of tradition can be dropped or suffer violence. Jesus' full revelation in regard to the complete equality of women and men was proclaimed theologically in the writings of Paul—in Christ there is neither male nor female—and was perhaps lived in the earliest Christian communities in a fullness not again achieved. Perhaps the time is near at hand. The role of Mary and her exaltation have been proclaimed in ever greater fullness. Now is the time to see her first *among* women, one with all women, who share fully in her call to enjoy preeminent intimacy and discipleship, to mother the whole Church community, to mother the whole Christ who we are.

There is within this living tradition of the Christian faithful certain phenomena which some would prefer to ignore completely. Yet the apparitions of the Blessed Virgin Mary have powerfully marked the piety of many of the faithful and have in some instances come into the formal liturgical worship of the Church; for example, the Feast of Our Lady of Lourdes. Not to look at those apparitions which have been thoroughly researched, some for many decades, before they were declared "worthy of belief" and continue to be researched and which have profoundly touched the Christian lives of millions, is to succumb to a prejudice and to present an incomplete picture of Mary as Christian tradition presents her to us. Tradition did not end with the Apostles, nor with the Mothers and Fathers of the Church, nor in the Middle Ages. Tradition goes on, with each of us bearing the responsibility to receive the Christian heritage as fully as we can, to let it live in our lives, receiving the impression and enrichment the Spirit will give it in and through us, and then to pass it on as fully and integrally as we possibly can. We are all part of the tradition, for better or for worse. We all have our contribution to make. Mary has continued to make her contribution by special "visits" to the Church on earth and the seers have made and are making theirs by receiving these visits with openness and sharing them as they can. The millions responding to their message are also making their contribution, especially those who have allowed these experiences to change their lives physically (some of the most carefully researched and fully attested miracles in the history of the Christian tradition have occurred in the waters at

Lourdes) and spiritually, making them more like Mary as dedicated disciples of Christ her Son.

The living Christian tradition does go on. Will someday the twentieth century be looked back to as part of the "early Church"? Perhaps. It makes sense if we consider how long it has taken for the creation to prepare for the coming of Christ.

Yet we do live under a nuclear cloud. We could end our race and just about all the other living species on our globe with the arsenals that stand ready to act. Perhaps evolution is accelerating. Grace abounds yet more. We are in the age of spiritual evolution. The key to spiritual evolution is the transformation of consciousness: "Let this mind be in you which was in Christ Jesus." It is the full acquisition, as a conscious reality, as the context of our response to life, of the fullness of the Revelation, the expression of God within the creation that is Jesus and that was revealed to us. This consciousness necessarily includes the total equality of all humans who find their ultimate purely human expression in the woman who is rightly called the Holy Mother of God. As she mothers God in an inconceivable substantial reality so are we each to mother God in inconceivable participative reality in ourselves and in each other. In this ultimate meaning, the consummation of the whole creative evolutionary process, sex and gender distinctions, beautiful and significant as they are, can in no wise be causes of inequality. All possess the same potency to this divine activation.

It is only when all things are truly ours and we are Christ's and he is God's, when Christ is all things in all, that the course of tradition will be complete. And only then will we know the fullness of the meaning of the woman from Nazareth. For the present, we seek to access as fully as we can all that has been given to us.

Two Thousand Bishops

Roman Catholics these days tend to think in terms of the Second Vatican Council. That gathering of over two thousand of the world's bishops was a moment of breakthrough, a new beginning, a second Pentecost for old Mother Church. However, as the Church opened for dialogue, its partners in dialogue could not help but be affected by its new spirit. Indeed, a charismatic movement broke many barriers and opened many hearts. Fundamentalists discovered that Catholics also love Jesus. Something was also discovered in the midst of common sufferings in a new age of martyrs. Shared studies have produced new translations of the Sacred Scripture and new lectionaries, allowing us to listen to the Word of God together. Even particulars of the liturgical renewal have passed across sectarian lines.

Some catholics have seen the council as the beginning of the end of marian devotions. Liturgical renewal has supplanted many of the devotions popular in recent centuries. Renewal of church buildings has swept away statues and pictures with their votive lamps and flowers. Priests preach more from the Scriptures; the Bible is the common text in catechism classes.

However, I think if we listen attentively to the Spirit speaking through the Second Vatican Council we will discover a solid and chaste basis for a strong marian devotion, a basis which may be able to be shared more widely in the Christian community, leading to a more widespread, deeper and more solid devotion to the Holy Mother of God.

A decisive note in the council was the decision to place the primary conciliar teaching on Mary within the Constitution on the Church. Mary was not to stand apart but within the community of

Across the Tiber

the disciples of Jesus. She is in the Church and of the Church, albeit mother of the Church as mother of its Head.

In the first major document of the council, the whole tone of the mariology of the Second Vatican is set forth in one rather succinct paragraph. Speaking of the liturgical year, the Constitution on the Sacred Liturgy notes that in celebrating the mysteries of Christ, we honor Mary precisely as mother with a special love. So it is within our response to Christ that our response to Mary comes. It is special and it is a thing of love because Christ, the perfect Son, had a special love for this mother. The text notes that this is so because Mary is "inseparably" linked with her Son's work. The link has two aspects and is preeminent in both: Mary is the most excellent fruit of Christ's redeeming and, in that, she is the perfect image of what we desire and hope to be.

Because it sums it all up so well, let me quote the paragraph:

> In celebrating the annual cycle of the mysteries of Christ, Holy Church honors the Blessed Mary, Mother of God, with a special love. She is inseparably linked with her Son's saving work. In her the Church admires and exalts the most excellent fruit of redemption, and joyfully contemplates, as in a faultless image, that which it itself desires and hopes to be.

The most important document to emerge from the Council is the Constitution on the Church, *Lumen gentium, (The Light of the Nations)* linked with its pastoral complement, the Constitution on the Church in the Modern World, *Gaudium et spes (Joy and Hope).* It is not surprising then that the Council's most complete teaching on Mary is found in this doctrinal text.

I have already spoken of how much a challenge it was to the council fathers to discern how best to treat of Mary. There was a strong movement to have a separate document on Mary. But a wiser part argued that Mary's true role would be better brought out if she found her place within the text on the Church, the Pilgrim People of God. Thus there was added to the constitution an eighth and final chapter comprising five sections, some eighteen paragraphs.

The chapter begins with the oldest New Testament text to speak of Mary, the one in St. Paul's Epistle to the Galatians (4:4): "when the fullness of time came, God sent his Son, born of a woman . . . that we might receive the adoption of sons." Mary is, first of all, before all, *woman.* We have seen what the Scriptures have had to say about *the* woman, the powerful mother of the faithful. The text here, in the way it is quoted by the fathers of the council, seeks to bring out this maternal role of Mary. While Christ's redemptive work makes us one with him in his eternal sonship, it also, by his dying request, makes us one with him in his being Son of Mary. The text then immediately quotes the Nicene-Constantinople Creed—"He for us, and for our salvation, came down from heaven, and was incarnated by the Holy Spirit from the Virgin Mary"—and the Roman Canon or Anaphora, one of our oldest liturgical texts, as it speaks of "the glorious ever Virgin Mary, Mother of God and of our Lord Jesus Christ." Thus is affirmed the inseparable link between the Sacred Scriptures and Tradition as the source by which we know Mary and her role within the Church.

In its Constitution on the Divine Revelation, the only other doctrinal constitution coming from Vatican II, the council sought to clarify how these two sources flow together to give us the fullest possible understanding of revelation:

> Sacred Tradition and Sacred Scripture, then, are bound closely together, and communicate one with the other. For both of them, flowing out from the same divine well-spring, come together in some fashion to form one thing, and move towards the same goal. Sacred Scripture is the speech of God as it is put down in writing under the breath of the Holy Spirit. And Tradition transmits in its entirety the Word of God which has been entrusted to the apostles by Christ the Lord and Holy Spirit . . . thus it comes about that the Church does not draw her certainty about all revealed truths from the Holy Scriptures alone. Hence, both Scripture and Tradition must be accepted and honored with equal feelings of devotion and reverence. Sacred Tradition and Sacred Scripture make up a single deposit of the Word of God, which is entrusted to the Church.

It also speaks of the development of doctrine, of which we spoke in the last chapter:

> The Tradition that comes from the apostles makes progress in the Church, with the help of Holy Spirit. There is a growth in insight into the realities and words that are being passed on. This comes about in various ways. It comes through the con-

templation and study of believers who ponder these things in their hearts. It comes from the intimate sense of spiritual realities which they experience. And it comes from the preaching of those who have received, along with their right of succession in the episcopate, the sure charism of truth. Thus, as the centuries go by, the Church is always advancing towards the plenitude of divine truth, until eventually the words of God are fulfilled in it.

I am tempted at this point just to quote at length from the eighth chapter of *The Light of the Nations (Lumen gentium)*. It is so rich and so richly packed that every sentence of it deserves to be pondered in the heart. For that reason I will include it in an Appendix.

In a few pages it seeks to sum up the whole of the content of marian tradition and succeeds well in its endeavor.

Beginning with Mary's unique and most exalted role as mother of God, she is related to the sublime Trinity as "beloved daughter," "mother" and "temple of Holy Spirit." "But, being of the race of Adam, she is at the same time also united to all those who are to be saved." These are the two poles of all our consideration of Mary, "who occupies a place in the Church which is the highest after Christ and closest to us." The council document, coming at the end of an era that sought to exalt Mary as much as possible, while it seeks to redress the exaggerations that this attitude fostered, still gives its weight in the direction of the pole of divinity in Mary's regard. This is good if we can only grasp strongly Mary's identity with us and realize that this is where the emphasis should be placed in the lives of all of us who are with Mary beneficiaries of the redeeming activity of her Son, our Brother and Lord—that we too have been brought into intimate relations with the Trinity as sons and daughters of the Father, one with *the* Son, living temples of Holy Spirit.

The fathers set forth their aim as being to bring out "painstakingly" Mary's relation to Christ and to his Mystical Body, which we are, and our duties toward her. Pointing to the prophecies to be found in the Old Testament (Genesis 3:15 and Isaiah 7:14) the text rather emphasizes that Mary "stands out among the poor and humble of the Lord, who confidently hope for and receive salvation from him." Mary's New Testament history is well summarized, preceded by her being appropriately preserved from all sin even from the time of conception and culminating in her being exalted by her Son as "queen over all things."

When the fathers come to consider Mary's role within the Church, they first profess apostolic faith: "In the words of the apostle there is but one mediator: 'for there is but one God and one mediator of God and men, the man Christ Jesus, who gave himself a redemption for all.' " Mary's function "in no way obscures or diminishes this unique mediation of Christ"; it "rests on his mediation, depends entirely on it and draws all its power from it. It does not hinder in any way the immediate union of the faithful with Christ but on the contrary fosters it." A council marked by ecumenical concern seeks first of all to alleviate the fears which circumscribe the attitude of many Christians in their approach to Mary.

Mary's role begins with her special cooperation with the work of redemption: her free consent to be mother, her conceiving, bearing, birthing and nurturing Christ, sharing his life and sufferings. Her cooperation continues in heaven by way of "her manifold intercession" by which she "continues to bring us the gifts of eternal salvation." Therefore she is given such titles as Advocate, Helper, Benefactress and Mediatrix.

In seeking to explain these titles, which have a long history, the document first affirms the uniqueness of Christ. Then it draws parallels in the way the priesthood of Christ is shared by ministers (priests and those preparing for the priesthood are directed by the council to look to Mary in a special way) and the faithful and the way the essential goodness of God is participated in by his creation: "sharing in the one source." "The Church does not hesitate to profess this subordinate role of Mary." Mary is present and active in the life of the faithful to help us "more closely adhere to the Mediator and Redeemer."

Appealing to St. Ambrose—the conciliar text frequently appeals to the early Fathers—the council affirms that Mary is a "type" of the Church: virgin and mother, who by faith, love and obedience brings forth Christ under the activity of Holy Spirit. But while Mary did this perfectly without sin, the community of the People of God, the Church, is made up of sinful members. Thus we look to Mary as model in our life and in our missions.

The fourth section of the chapter opens with the basic statement in regard to honoring Mary: "Mary has by grace been exalted above all angels and human beings to a place second only to her Son, as the most holy mother of God who was involved in the mysteries of Christ: she is rightly honored by a special cult in the Church." The paragraph goes on to state that this cult "differs essentially from the cult of adoration" which is offered to God and Christ. While liturgical cult and the reverence of images which are traditional in the Christian community and sustained by earlier councils are fostered there is an exhortation that "strongly urges theologians and preachers of the Word of God to be careful to refrain as much from all false exaggeration as from too summary an attitude in considering the special dignity of the Mother of God." True devotion is defined: it "consists neither in sterile or transitory affection, nor in a certain vain credulity, but proceeds from true faith, by which we are led to recognize the excellence of the Mother of God, and we are moved to a filial love towards our mother and to the imitation of her virtues."

Mary is a sign of hope and comfort for us pilgrims. She already possesses the glory which is the image and beginning of the glory of the whole People of God. In this hope the document ends with a prayer

> that she, who aided the beginnings of the Church by her prayers, may now, exalted as she is above all the angels and saints, intercede before her Son in the fellowship of all the saints, until all families of people, whether they are honored with the title of Christian or whether they still do not know the Saviour, may be happily gathered together in peace and harmony into one People of God, for the glory of the Most Holy and Undivided Trinity.

The Decree on the Renewal of Religious Life ends with a similar prayer.

The Second Vatican Council in the course of its documents has given us virtually a new litany of the Blessed Virgin Mary, bringing forth from its treasures, as a wise householder, titles old and new:

Adiutrix	Helper
Alma Redemptoris Mater	Gracious Mother of the Redeemer
Ancilla Domini	Handmaid of the Lord
Auxiliatrix	Helper
Auxilium Christianorum	Helper of Christians
Auxilium Episcoporum	Helper of Bishops
Dei Genetrix	Mother of God

Deipara	Godbearer
Exemplar Ecclesiae	Example for the Church
Filia Adam	Daughter of Adam
Filia benedicta Ecclesiae	Blest Daughter of the Church
Filia Patris praedilecta	Chosen Daughter of the Father
Filia Sion praeclara	Illustrious Daughter of Sion
Genetrix Dei Filii	Mother of the Son of God
Gratia plena	Full of Grace
Imago limpidissima Dei	Most Limpid Image of God
Immaculata Virgo	Immaculate Virgin
Immunis ab omni peccato	Sinless One
Mater Aeterni Sacerdotis	Mother of the Eternal Priest
Mater Dei	Mother of God
Mater Domini	Mother of the Lord
Mater Ecclesiae	Mother of the Church
Mater hominum	Mother of Men
Mater Jesu	Mother of Jesus
Mater membrorum Christi	Mother of the Members of Christ
Mater nostra	Our Mother
Mater Redemptoris	Mother of the Redeemer
Mater Salvatoris	Mother of the Savior
Mater virginialis	Virgin Mother
Mater viventium	Mother of the Living
Mediatrix	Mediatrix
Membrum supereminens Ecclesiae	Supereminent Member of the Church
Mulier idealis	Ideal Woman
Nova Eva	New Eve
Patrona Apostolatus laicorum	Patron of the Lay Apostolate
Regina Apostolorum	Queen of the Apostles
Regina universorum	Queen of the Universe
Sacrarium Spiritus Sancti	Temple of Holy Spirit
Salus Populi Romani	Salvation of the Roman People
Sanctissima	Most Holy One
Semper Virgo	Ever Virgin
Signum certae spei	Sign of Sure Hope
Signum solatii	Sign of Consolation
Socia generosa Redemptoris	Generous Consort of the Redeemer
Typus Ecclesiae	Type of the Church
Virgo beatissima	Most Blessed Virgin
Virgo Nazarethana	Virgin of Nazareth

It is this last title we might have liked to see developed more fully: Virgin of Nazareth—woman of time and place, woman of her People. But the time was not yet ripe for that.

In fact, I think many of us, although we may be in total sympathy with all that is set forth by the council, yet find it painful to read this rather desiccated abstract presentation so lacking in those rich, warm qualities we identify with the feminine. I recently wrote a book on my friend Thomas Merton. It was a very painful experience. Lacking his literary endowments, I could not produce a text no matter how true its content that would reflect the lightsome way in which he was able to express the deepest of divine and human realities. I suspect that those who were crafting the council document on Mary never gave a thought to trying to make it a statement that would reflect something of Mary's own beauty and spirit. We have to be big enough to accept it as the very prosaic poetry of a generally senior group whose lives and relationships, even with Mary, have been largely guided by and nourished by the abstractions of an almost exclusively scholastic theology.

Tradition has moved on since the Second Vatican Council. In a rapidly evolving world it is essentially human consciousness that is evolving. The handing on becomes more rapid and the changes more profound. Less than ten years after the council Pope Paul VI, who presided over most of its deliberations, published an encyclical letter concerning devotion to Mary: *Marialis cultus* (February 2, 1974). In the opening paragraphs of his letter, the Pontiff acknowledges this rapid ongoing evolution:

> In our time, the changes that have occurred in social behavior, people's sensibilities, literary and artistic modes of expression, and in the communications media have also influenced the manifestations of religious sentiment. Certain practices that not long ago seemed suitable for expressing the religious sentiment of individuals and Christian communities seem today inadequate or unsuitable because they are linked with social and cultural patterns of the past. In many places people are seeking new ways of expressing the unchangeable relationship of creatures with their Creator, of children with their Father. This may cause temporary confusion in some people. But anyone who, with trust in God, reflects upon these phenomena discovers that many tendencies of modern piety (for example,

the interiorization of religious sentiment) are meant to play their part in the development of Christian piety in general and devotion to the Blessed Virgin in particular. Thus our own time, faithfully attentive to tradition and to the progress of theology and other disciplines, will make its own contribution of praise to her whom, according to her own prophetic words, all generations will call blessed.

We do not want to be a generation that fails to honor the holy Virgin or to call her blessed in our own proper way. With a certain courage and detachment we need to give appropriate expression to our experience of Mary and our homage in response to that experience. At the same time we realize what we offer is for today, to be passed on for others to reform and reshape for tomorrow.

The text of the Constitution on the Church of the Second Vatican Council was indeed a compromise text. It needed to be to serve a Church where the members are at all different places in their evolution. It did seek to return from the independent mariology that developed in the last century with its maximization to a more ecclesiological perspective, seeing Mary fully in and of the Church. The careful research and consultations that went on in preparation for the solemn formulation in 1950 of the doctrine of the glorious assumption of Mary body and soul into heaven led to a return to the patristic sources and a greater sobriety in regard to the Virgin. The development from those sources which we would like to see, bringing out Mary's full humanness and womanliness and her contribution to the work of salvation and the life of the Church as woman, is taking place now. But with difficulty. Ours is still very much an androcentric church, dominated by a patriarchal mind that places the female under the male. Within such a mentality it is not possible for the most important collaborator of the Redeemer, the first of the disciples, to emerge, fulfilling her role precisely as a woman. Something of her humanity has to be lost in a divinity that will cloak her femininity. The full historical reality of Mary, *the Woman,* cannot emerge within the tradition of a male-dominated Church. Such a development of doctrine must await that evolution of human consciousness that will have the courage to accept woman for all that she truly is, the helpmate of man, like unto himself, both images of God in every way equal. Then will we be free enough to see fully Mary, blessed among woman.

Mary Appearing

Visions and heavenly visitation are certainly not something foreign to the historical roots of our faith. The Lord himself, often in the form of angels, came to our father Abraham. In such an angelic form he wrestled with patriarch Jacob. Gideon, the judge, and Balaam, the prophet, and so many others, right down to Mary's husband and Mary herself, they, too, were called forth and guided in their mission by messengers from heaven. Peter and Paul had visions to instruct them, as they broke from expected ways and reached out ever further to bring the faith of Christ to the nations. Morton Kelsey has estimated that if we removed from the New Testament all the references to extraordinary experiences of God— dreams, visions and miracles—we would have only half the text remaining. Perhaps that is a generous estimate, but Peter, under the influence of the Holy Spirit on that first Pentecost, the birthday of the Church, prophesied of it (borrowing the words of an earlier prophet): Your young men shall see visions and your old men shall dream dreams.

The first reports of marian visitations are woven into the rich fabric of early Christian times when historical fact and legend came together to create the clothing of the faith. These reports did not see the need to distinguish between fact and legend so long as they served the true faith. They were, in time, enshrined in the prayer life, both liturgical and devotional, of the Christian people.

On August 5, for example, we celebrate the ancient feast of Our Lady of Snows. This story goes back to the fifth century. Mary appeared to the patrician John and his wife (what better times were those when it was deemed most proper that Mary should appear to a married couple together—not just to the man of the house as the head, or the woman as the pious one, but to the two whom God had made one in his sacramental love), telling them to build in her honor the great church they would find outlined in snow on the morrow. Indeed miraculous, snow in Rome on an August day. St. Mary Major, the primal church of Mary in Rome, stands as the centuries-old witness to this apparition.

We have all seen pictures of Mary handing the rosary to St. Dominic and the scapular to St. Simon Stock. Feasts honor Our Lady of the Rosary and Our Lady of Mount Carmel. For centuries, these sacramentals came to catholic children with first Communion and remained an important part of their devotional life till death— the rosary in their hands and the scapular on their shoulders, mute prayers ensuring safe passage under the watchful eye of Mary. The latter apparition to Simon has perhaps more chance of authenticity than the former but neither were reported in the lives of the respective saints until long after their deaths.

* * *

The earliest apparitions that are reported to us with a ring of historical authenticity are those which took place on the hill of Tepeyac, just outside Mexico City, in December 1531. Christianity had come to the shores of the Americas less than forty years before. It came as the religion of conquerors who were not only smashing ancient cultures but also seeking to wipe out the indigenous religion of the conquered people. Mary appeared on the side of the oppressed.

Juan Diego, an Aztec peasant who had already embraced the new faith with exceptional piety, was hastening to mass. It was a Saturday, the day on which Mary is especially honored, and, in this case, December 9, 1531, the day after the celebration of the Feast of the Conception of the Virgin. Mary came to the little man as one of his own, a short, swarthy Aztec maiden, an appearance probably not much different from her actual native appearance as an oriental Jew. She spoke the indian's native dialect, Nahuatl. Her message was simple and reassuring: I am your merciful mother; to you and to all the inhabitants of this earth, to all who love me, invoke me and confide in me; I listen to their lamentations and remedy all their miseries, afflictions and sorrows. A Jewish mother with her oppressed children. To give them a rallying point and to make clear her claim to replace the mother-goddess, Tonantzin, who was formerly worshiped on that hill, Mary sent Juan to the new bishop of

Mexico City with instructions that a church be built for her on the hill.

Juan, with courageous simplicity, went immediately to the bishop. It says something for this Spanish nobleman, Don Juan de Zumárraga, that he was accessible to his flock, even the poorest and most humble, and kept a translator at his side so that he could hear them. Don Juan was understandably somewhat skeptical about Juan's story, but kindly disposed to the indian. He promised to hear the little man again sometime. Juan returned immediately to the merciful mother. He found her waiting. And he was told to return to the bishop to renew her demand.

The next morning, Sunday, the tenth of December, Juan retraced his steps to the bishop's house. Again he was received with kindness by the prelate. After listening to the message, the bishop asked for some sign that this was indeed the Mother of God who was making this demand of him. Mary had given her name to Juan: Perpetual and perfect Virgin Mary, holy Mother of the true God through whom everything lives, the Creator and Master of heaven and earth —it was to Juan's uncle that she subsequently gave the name Our Lady of Guadalupe. Juan immediately reported back to Mary, who promised to give him the requested sign on the morrow.

On the eleventh Juan could not leave his house. His uncle, who lived with him, was very sick. Through that night the old man's condition worsened. On the morning of the twelfth Juan decided he must go seek a priest to minister to his dying uncle. The little man tried to escape an encounter with Mary, aware that he had not come the day before as he had promised. He did not want to delay getting the priest. But Mary caught him on the back path he was taking and told him she would take care of his uncle—which she did, appearing to him shortly after, curing him. Mary sent Juan to the top of the hill to gather roses—in December!—for the bishop. Mary arranged the roses herself in Juan's tilma, or cloak, and sent him on his way with the charge not to open his tilma, in which she had arranged the roses, until he was before the bishop.

The bishop's servants made it difficult for Juan to carry out Mary's command, but he succeeded. When he did open his tilma before the bishop, the roses cascaded out. There, before the eyes of all, was the remarkable image of Mary which to this day remains bright and fresh, allowing us to see the maiden who appeared to Juan. The miraculous image itself stands as a miracle to authenticate

Our Lady of Guadalupe

these apparitions. On rough maguey cloth, woven from the dried cactus, with no sizing or preparation, the image has amazed artists. It has remained free from any deterioration through more than four centuries in spite of the candleblack and clouds of incense that have ceaselessly surrounded it. The lively colors remain bright. Amazement was compounded when modern photography, with its powers of magnification, revealed in the pupil of Mary's eye the image of a little Indian, undoubtedly the Juanito she was gazing on.

Within two weeks of the last apparition of Mary to Juan the indians themselves built a chapel and the bishop brought back the tilma in solemn procession. According to estimates which may be somewhat generous, but nonetheless can not be too inflated, in the six years following upon the day when the Holy Mother of God showed herself to be one of them, some eight million indians were baptized into the faith of her Son. The image was a catechism for the Aztecs: it showed Mary, wearing the cross of salvation, crushing the ancient serpent; this typology of the evil one belonged to their tradition as well.

The bishop of Mexico City never issued a formal decree declaring the apparitions "worthy of belief" as would later become the practice in such cases. Was it necessary? In 1754 Pope Benedict XIV approved a mass and office in honor of Our Lady of Guadalupe which is still celebrated throughout the world on December 12.

It would be difficult to exaggerate the importance of these apparitions of Mary at Tepeyac in the first days of American Christianity. From the very beginning, Mary's presence has given dignity to the downtrodden, hope to the exploited and motivation to all the liberation movements. The degradation of a people and a civilization that was being perpetrated by the Spanish conquest is beyond description: political, economic, sexual, sociological, psychological and religious, it sought to destroy the very soul of the people. In the midst of all this there is this sudden irruption. An indian Queen of Heaven comes, blending together European and Nahuatl traditions concerning God. The indigenous population was called forth as active participants in the construction of the new religious culture. The oppressed had an important ally: "I vividly desire that a temple be built on this site, so that in it I can be present and give all my love, compassion, help and defense, for I am your most devoted mother . . . to hear your laments, and to remedy all your miseries, pains and sufferings."

As God came in the person of Moses to the oppressed in Egypt to lead them under his signs to freedom as his people, Mary came to the oppressed people of the Americas. Under her banner one nation after the other won its freedom in New Spain. Even in our time, the oppressed farmworkers march under her banners as they strike for freedom and dignity.

Through Mary, Jesus became incarnate in the New World, giving birth to a new church. For the indigenization and acculturation to which the Second Vatican Council summoned the churches of all nations, Mary set the example centuries before in Mexico when she appeared among the Aztecs as an Aztec. This indigenization will be successfully accomplished only if today's hierarchs can, like the bishop of Mexico City, Juan de Zumárraga, allow humble listening to bridge the gaps between class, race and culture. The dark-skinned indian woman, Our Lady of Guadalupe, stands in our midst to rebuke any racism and sexism, assuring the poor where God's option lies. When we can be humble enough to allow other cultures to make the contribution they can make, our faith will be able to shine forth with a new richness, a thing of unfading beauty like the image of Our Lady of Guadalupe.

This challenge is especially important for the United States Church today. Virtually a third of our membership is Hispanic. There needs to be a willingness to let the riches of the faith that these women and men have brought across the border be added to the heritage we already enjoy—true in this to the United States' heritage of being a melting pot where each immigrant culture has been able to bring its contribution. There stands before us the opportunity and the call for the United States Church to come to a new fullness of humanity and divinity. When we open the ears of our hearts, letting go of all our prejudices, accepting the people of the simple indian Maiden of Guadalupe as fully part of our Church in the United States and listening to their experience of God and of his mother, we will come to a new fullness of understanding and being, one that responds to the deepest longings of our hearts.

In 1945, Pope Pius XII proclaimed the Virgin of Guadalupe "Empress of America." It was the era of triumphalism in the Church. The title ill fits the humble woman depicted on the tilma of Juan Diego. It ill fits her message. She will always be to millions of native Americans, and to the immigrant population, too, simply, as she herself said, a most dear and merciful mother.

*   *   *

Nineteenth-century France was overwhelmingly blessed with heavenly visitations, which have spilled over into our century and into other nations. I will speak only of the relatively few that have been finally declared "worthy of belief" by a highly critical and demanding authority. While these visitations of Mary have much in common, there is nonetheless within them a rich variety, and a variety in their significance and impact.

If, on a warm summer's day when men are apt to have their shirts quite open, you walk along a busy street, you will see that one after another is wearing around his neck a chain and frequently an amulet or two is suspended from it. In the case of women, this is more perceptible the year round. If you were to examine the amulets worn by the catholic men you would find in very many cases they are wearing that medal which we call "miraculous."

Wearing amulets, just like using beads and receiving a garment of affiliation, is something quite natural to the human. We find these practices in every culture; they usually have a religious significance. Though the cross will always be the first sign, the most common amulet, among us Christians, our sacramentals have often come to have a special tie to the Blessed Virgin. In our tradition Mary is found providing for our very human need in this regard.

While there is some question whether Mary actually handed the first rosary to St. Dominic and the scapular to St. Simon, the apparitions at Paris in 1830 are clearly historical events. In this case, again, Mary's choice fell upon a most unlikely person to accomplish her mission: to give to the Church a new medal. About 11:30 on the night of July 18, Mary sent "a little boy" to awaken the postulant Catherine Labouré, with the message "The Blessed Virgin awaits you." Not only was Catherine on the lowest rung in the ladder of religious life, but she was a very simple young woman, largely unschooled, just learning to read and write. Perhaps only someone with her simplicity would have gotten up and followed the little messenger to the chapel and obeyed his instruction to kneel by the chaplain's chair in the sanctuary. That chair is still there for the devout to kneel by.

As Catherine knelt, Mary entered by a side door, bowed to the tabernacle and sat in the chair. Catherine drew nearer and rested her hands in Mary's lap. For two hours the postulant was instructed by her heavenly mother. Mary promised to give her a mission. With tears, Mary also foretold the sorrows that lay ahead for France, including the oppression by the Prussians in 1870. When Mary disappeared the child led Catherine back to her bed. It was 2 A.M.

Catherine had been told to share her experience only with her confessor, a young man of thirty. He did not give her any credence.

Four months later, on the twenty-seventh of November, while the novices were in chapel praying, Catherine again heard the sound of rustling silk that had marked Mary's entrance into the sanctuary in July. There was Mary, suspended in the air, to the right of the main altar. She was all in white, veiled, holding a golden globe in her hands. The globe was surmounted by a cross. Suddenly the globe was gone and there poured forth from Mary's gem-laden hands rays of light. An inner voice told Catherine these were graces Mary was transmitting to those who would accept them. Many were refusing.

Then the vision again shifted and Catherine was shown what was to be the front of a medal. Around Mary appeared in French the prayer: O Mary conceived without original sin, pray for us who have recourse to you. Catherine was told: Those who wear this medal blessed and say confidently this prayer will receive great graces and the constant protection of the mother of God. Then the reverse side of the medal was shown: the burning hearts of Jesus and Mary, an "M" surmounted by the cross, and an encircling twelve stars.

Again, Catherine's confessor greeted her message with disbelief. In the course of the ensuing year Mary appeared to Catherine three more times, complaining at the lack of progress in getting the medal made and distributed. Finally the chaplain spoke to the archbishop, who encouraged him to get the medal made, asking that he be given the first copy. A Parisian artisan was commissioned to make fifteen hundred medals. Before he could complete them there was demand for more. In three years a couple of million had been distributed and miracles were being reported on all sides. People hailed the "miraculous medal."

As Mary had requested, an altar was erected on the site of the apparition in the chapel of the Daughters of Charity on the Rue de Bac. Over it a statue depicting Mary holding the golden globe was to have been placed, but this was not done. So, in 1876, when she realized she was soon to die, Catherine told her superior of Our Lady's wishes in the matter and the statue was commissioned. It was only at this time that the sisters came to know to whom among them

Mary had given this gift of the miraculous medal. Some fifty-six years after her death, Catherine's precious remains were placed beneath the altar of the apparitions.

As Mary gave a picture and a sanctuary at Guadalupe, so she gave a medal and a shrine in inner-city Paris to convey the same message in a way very natural to the children to whom she was speaking. She is a mother with us, to care for us. It is the message of Cana and Calvary. Today we see many men wearing golden chains around their necks without anything on them. I think of one of my young friends from Paris. His chain came with a golden miraculous medal. He still wears the medal at times. But more often he wears only the chain. Because he wants to do things and be in places where he does not want his mother to be present. Mary has never forsaken her children, but we too often seek to escape her watchful care—to our own detriment and sorrow.

* * *

La Salette, Pontmain, Knock—these apparitions seem to be nothing more than Mary coming to console her suffering and oppressed children. At La Salette, the woman who usually smiled at her children wept and wept before she smiled. At Pontmain she came to a devout village that was in terror, expecting at any moment to be overrun by enemy forces. The inhabitants were filled with fear for their sons and husbands and fathers who had been called to the fighting. Within days the Prussians inexplicably withdrew and soon negotiated a peace. Ireland, so beaten down with religious persecution and deadly famine, saw a million of her sons depart for foreign lands. On a cold rainy night Mary stood silently in the remote village, with her husband and Child and the beloved disciple. No word was uttered, only a reassuring, loving presence.

* * *

It was Lourdes that became the site of the outstanding apparitions of the nineteenth century. Again, Mary chose one of the least. Bernadette's father was unemployed, handicapped and just out of jail. The family was crowded into the back room of an abandoned jail and not even able to afford the expected rent for that. Among the poverty-stricken brood, Bernadette was the weakest, the asthmatic. Yet she was Mary's chosen. A simple, unlettered girl, who was to display great courage and dignity.

Mary came to Bernadette for the first time on a cold winter's day, February 2, 1858, in what was sort of the garbage dump of the village, a place where swine were pastured. Mary smiled, said little, prayed the rosary with her child. That was on Thursday. Bernadette returned on Sunday and it was much the same. The following Thursday, instigated by a well-meaning widow, Bernadette asked the lady to write her name. Mary replied that it was not necessary and asked Bernadette to have the graciousness to return each day for fifteen days. Mary spoke the girl's native patois. She added: I do not promise to make you happy in this world but in the next. Bernadette would have a lot to suffer before the apparitions were over and on through her short life.

A week later, after asking Bernadette to give herself to penitence and prayer for conversions and instructing her in little acts of penance, Mary directed her to dig in the grotto. The miraculous waters began to flow. The first miracle was reported a couple days later. On March 2 Mary told Bernadette to go to the priests and ask for a procession and a chapel. The pastor wanted to know who this was who wanted a procession. Bernadette asked the heavenly visitor's name again and again, receiving only a smile in response. Finally, Mary told Bernadette her name. The girl did not understand, but she repeated the name continually as she made her way to the presbytery: I am the Immaculate Conception. How could an unlettered peasant know that the Pope in faraway Rome had, four years previous, solemnly proclaimed the immaculate conception of the virgin Mary.

Today, each day, some twenty-seven thousand gallons of water pour forth from the spring Bernadette unearthed and an average of three hundred and fifty thousand people come to drink or to bathe. Thousands of cures have been attributed to the water. But a most rigorous medical committee has so far formally recognized only sixty-four as being undoubtedly miraculous. Most who come seeking a physical cure do not receive what they came for. Rather they find something more precious: a deep inner peace, a joy and meaning in suffering, a compassion for others. In a word, they receive a share in Mary's own inner dispositions. A motherly love that changed a garbage dump into one of Christendom's most beautiful and faith-and-hope-filled sanctuaries assures those who would heed her and are open to her maternal care that the most wretched of human existences can be turned into a thing of beauty through a mother's love.

* * *

There have been many, many apparitions reported in our century. One author has counted 232 in thirty-two countries from 1923 to 1975. Relatively few have been seriously investigated, very few officially rejected, and only three groups so far have been declared "worthy of belief." Two of these occurred in neighboring areas in Belgium, Beauraing and Banneux, within a short time of each other: 1932–33. These were consoling visits to unlikely children (one of whom is still living), given at a time when things looked very dark in Europe, a time of worldwide depression.

The apparitions that have had the greatest impact and continue to speak powerfully to us are those that took place near Fátima, Portugal, in 1917. Again, Mary chose children of the poorest sort, little shepherds; God loves shepherds. But this time the children were carefully prepared for the coming visits of the Immaculate One.

In the spring of 1916 an angel, appearing as a young man of fifteen, came and taught the three children, by example as much as by word, how to pray. The children were instinctively drawn into silence (they never told anyone about these angelic visits; Lucia Santos, the oldest of the three, revealed them only after the apparitions of the Blessed Virgin were declared "worthy of belief" in 1930), into a fervent and prolonged practice of the prayer of adoration the angel taught them and into self-denial. On the second visit of the angel, in midsummer, their heavenly instructor exhorted them to offer up prayer and sacrifices to the Most High, Lucia asked very simply: How are we to make sacrifices? The angel's answer is important, for Mary will be asking us for sacrifices in reparation for our sin. "Make everything you do a sacrifice and offer it as an act of reparation for the sins by which he is offended and in supplication for the conversion of sinners. Bring peace to your country in this way . . . Above all, accept and bear in submission the sufferings sent you by our Lord." We are not asked to do extraordinary or special things but to bring an inner disposition to all that we already do.

In the fall the angel gave the two youngest seers their first communion. It had been a relatively short time since the saintly Pius X had urged a return to early first communion. Lucia had been able to receive at the age of six. But the others, Francisco Marto, age eight, and his sister, Jacinta, age six, had not yet had the privilege. The Eucharist was to play a more central role at Fátima than it had in any previous marian apparition.

The angel, who identified himself as the Angel of Peace, had told the children that "the hearts of Jesus and Mary have designs for you." It was in the following May that these designs began to be realized.

At Fátima there was a bit of drama in the way Mary came each time: at full noon, with a flash of lightning, in a glowing ball descending from heaven. Yet on her first appearance Mary immediately sought to quiet the children's fears. It was Sunday, the thirteenth of May, when Mary first came. She asked the children to come on the thirteenth of each month for six months. She also asked them if they were willing to suffer in reparation and for conversions. She exhorted them to pray the rosary. (Later she would meet with Jacinta in the parish church and instruct her how to do it properly, meditating on the fifteen mysteries.)

In June, Mary spoke of her Immaculate Heart and showed it to the children. She foretold the early deaths of the two youngest. Curiously, Francisco could never hear anything the Virgin said and it had to be relayed to him by the girls.

The following month Mary declared herself Our Lady of the Rosary and asked that we pray the rosary daily for peace. She opened to the children a frightening vision of hell, foretold the Second World War, asked that the Russian people be consecrated to her care and asked that we receive communion on the first Saturday of each month, making reparation to her Immaculate Heart.

Mary's August visit was impeded when the public authorities kidnapped the children. Undaunted, Mary came to the three on the nineteenth in nearby Valinki. It was in September that Mary promised not only to delight the children with special apparitions but to give a great sign to all the people.

Some seventy thousand gathered in the Cove da Iria on October 13, in spite of a constant heavy downpour of rain. All was mud. Lucia's mother still did not believe and railed at her daughter. The Marto family lamented the complete destruction of their farm and garden land in the Cova by the mob. Mary came as usual. She delighted the children with visions of Jesus and of St. Joseph. Mary herself modeled, as it were, some of her own favorite "poses": the Mother of Sorrows and the Queen of Carmel. She asked that a chapel be constructed in the Cova, dedicated to her as the Lady of the Rosary. All were exhorted to pray the rosary; this would bring an end to war.

Then came the promised sign. Lucia had told the people to close their umbrellas at the beginning of Mary's visit. All were thoroughly soaked. Suddenly, the clouds opened and a leaden sun, one that the naked eye could regard, began its famous "dance." It spun around, throwing off lights of all colors that colored all in sight. Then it zigzagged crazily, moving toward the earth, inciting terror—not only among the crowd in the Cova but in towns many miles away. The performance was repeated three times. Then a beautiful sunny day broke forth and all found themselves and everything else perfectly dry. Now, even Lucia's mother believed.

This spectacle seems a little out of character for the Mary we know and as she has appeared in the Gospels and in the many preceding apparitions. Perhaps Mary was a bit desperate to get our attention, as the time is short, the danger to the human family great. Back in 1917 the horrors of the Second World War, which Mary foretold, were unimaginable: the dawning of the Atomic Age.

Pope Pius XII, who was actually being consecrated a bishop in Rome at the very time Mary was first appearing in Fátima, consecrated the world to the Immaculate Heart of Mary in 1942. Ten years later he specifically consecrated the Russian people. In 1964 Pope Paul VI renewed this consecration. Finally, in 1982 Pope John Paul II went to Fátima for the sixty-fifth anniversary of the first apparition and the first of his own near-assassination and, in union with the bishops of the world, "collegially" consecrated the world and Russia to Mary Immaculate.

* * *

Since 1981, Mary is reported to be appearing daily in a little Yugoslavian town, Medjugorje. There she has said this is the last time she will be coming to earth. She has come night after night to repeat substantially the same message: prayer—especially the rosary—and reparation, prayer for peace. She speaks of herself as the Queen of Peace. Choosing six quite ordinary children, poor enough and living under the oppression of a communist dictatorship, Mary has appeared as more of a mother than ever before. The youngest,

Jokov, age ten, has received special attention as Mary has taken him apart and sat down with him to talk at length. She scolds Yvon when he comes late from soccer and has not taken time to wash up. She has been very demanding with these children. While she usually talks with them for only a few minutes, the prayers before and after, including the full rosary and the mass, usually last all of three hours. Besides this, the children are expected to spend an hour a day praying at home and to fast on bread and water on Wednesdays and Fridays. All the notoriety—there are thousands present almost every evening—and all the religion do not seem to have affected the children, who are marked only by their ordinariness and goodness. The older girls, reaching twenty-one, no longer enjoy the nightly visits and one has moved to the city for employment. Recently, the older boy, Yvon, has been inducted into the army. He had had to drop out of the seminary but still hopes to be a Franciscan. Vicka is now afflicted with a brain tumor and often must stay at home; Mary comes to visit her there while she visits with the others at the priests' house.

* * *

There is a wide variety certainly in these fascinating stories. Yet there is a common denominator, in fact a number of them.

Most fundamental is Mary's loving care. She is still the Jewish mother at Cana who wants to take care of things, take care of her children. She is the woman who stood at the cross, knows what her Son has suffered, knows her motherly role. The response to such love must take the form of reparation. In some way, we need to make up for what our sin has caused, the sorrow and pain in the hearts of Jesus and Mary, our killing wars and all forms of human oppression. Peace among her children is a constant concern of this mother who at times names herself the Queen of Peace. At Pontmain, to those oppressed by war, she was Our Lady of Hope.

In an age when we are more aware of the social implications of the Gospels, we see Mary making strong social statements in deeds more than in words. Mary's option, like that of her Son, is clearly for the poor and oppressed. At Banneux she declares: "I am the Virgin of the Poor." In these modern times there is no claim for her having appeared to the rich. Rather, her predilection is for the most innocent of victims, the children of the oppressed. If we go today to Fátima, we can visit the humble homes of the three children, still used by Lucia's sister and the Marto children's brother Juan with his family: small, thatched roof, dirt floor. We will still find the families in the evening eating the same bowl of porridge. The poverty is bleak but not as bleak as that of the prison in which Bernadette lived. It is perhaps difficult for us to make an objective judgment whether the oppression of the supposedly God-fearing Spanish in Mexico was worse than that of the godless regimes in Portugal and in today's Yugoslavia.

There is a concrete practicality about Mary. She wants in each case to establish a rallying place for her children, a church or a chapel, and she marks it with some distinctive sign: a unique image, a health-giving spring. Her message of perduring love is made to perdure. Where oppression prevents this, she is adaptable. At Medjugorje when her children were barred from the mountain she first chose, she went with them to the church. When they could no longer use this building, Mary didn't hesitate to join them in the pastor's study. On particular occasions when civil authorities took the children away, she followed along.

I am also deeply impressed by Mary's wholehearted willingness to adapt herself to different peoples and cultures. In Mexico she appeared as Juan Diego might well expect his mother to appear. To the children in Europe she came with a Caucasian visage we have so grown accustomed to in our images of the mother of God, and the long flowing robe and the veil. The colorful garb at La Salette, while unusual in comparison to Mary's other appearances, seemed quite natural to the two children. When she spoke, she used the seers' language, whatever be the dialect or patois. Except for the case when Bernadette sought a response for another, Mary spoke in simple terms which her simple children could understand. After hearing the stories from these various apparitions, no one need fear approaching Mary and speaking to her in whatever way is natural.

Holiness does not seem to have been an essential mark among the seers. Some have become saints and are even canonized. But others went on to lead lives that were quite ordinary and in some cases as mixed up as those of the worst of us. Maximin Giraud, one of the seers of La Salette, who came from an unhappy home— alcoholic father and uncaring stepmother—remained a wounded person. He tried the minor seminary for a time, but left and drifted about until he died at the early age of forty. His companion, Mélanie Mathieu, did not fare much better. She went in and out of a series of convents in different countries and finally died in her seventies, a lonely old woman living on a pension granted to her by a charitable bishop in Italy. Yet each one of these seers is a chosen child of Mary, the object of her special love. And they never lost that love, for that is the way with a mother's love.

There is a lot about the various apparitions that can cause one to wonder: why this one, why here, why this way? Why this motley crew of seers? They will create a most interesting coterie in heaven. Why over a railroad bridge, in a garbage dump, in Father's garden? Why so many times? Why so slow to name herself? Why so elusive at times? Why? Why? Why?

Yes, there are lots of questions and I realize that because of this some are very sensitive to giving any credence to these apparitions, especially those which have not yet been declared "worthy of belief" by the responsible bishops. The light they throw on Mary actually does not add anything essential to what we know from the Gospels and Tradition. They are wholly consonant with the Mary who is revealed there. So do we really need to pay any heed to these private revelations? Should we? I think, with all due prudence, we can attend to them and, indeed, neglect them to our own loss.

One day the disciples of John the Baptizer came to Jesus with a question from their master: Are you the one who is to come, or should we look for another? Jesus replied: Tell John what you hear and see: the blind see, the lame walk, . . . and the poor have the gospel preached to them. These were the signs to which our Lord appealed to authenticate his mission. These are the signs that have constantly surrounded these apparitions of his mother. At Lourdes, carefully studied miracles attest to the power present, while at almost all the other sites miracles are reported. La Salette and Banneux also have their healing springs. Moreover, there are other more particular signs. The beautiful tilma at Guadalupe is a continuous miracle. The cactus fibers which should have disintegrated after twenty or thirty years keep their original vigor after four and a half centuries. Seventy thousand and many more saw the sun dance at Fátima. There are innumerable miracles attributed to the medal of Paris.

The steadfast courage of the little seers in the face of all sorts of threats is in itself something to evoke our wonder. Bernadette was taken into custody and also threatened by the parish priest. Her own mother went after her with a stick, as Lucia's mother did to her. The civil authorities at Fátima took the little ones separately and threatened to boil them in oil. Childish imaginations must have raced with horrid scenes, yet they remained steadfast in their witness. The children at Medjugorje were also taken into custody and pursued at times. Where do young people find such courage in the face of authority, civil and ecclesiastical?

There is the continuous miracle of these places in themselves. Year after year, decade after decade, thousands and tens of thousands flock to them with faith—to these places otherwise meaningless (who ever heard of Fátima before 1917 or of the town of Lourdes in the Pyrenees before a Bernadette? where is Medjugorje and how do you get there?), out of the way, offering nothing else but a great poverty of accommodations at the end of a long and difficult journey. Yet those who come find something there that draws them back again and again. These places bring people to Jesus. Masses abound, communions are multiplied, multitudes seek reconciliation. The Sacrament is carried in procession—Jesus walks again among his people. Jesus uses his mother in all these places to bring his people to himself.

The Gospels are the story of Mary's Son. She is but a supporting member of the cast. Her own character has little opportunity to shine forth. In these later appearances, when she is more central, we can get a much fuller picture of her. Yet she is no different from the woman in the Gospels and wholly in character with her Son, his way of being and acting. She calls us back to the basic truths of faith and to the simple practices that respond to these. Mary reminds us of the dispositions that are necessary to receive the Word of God and enter into his Kingdom. At the same time she touches on the needs of the moment that weigh on the minds and hearts of her children and she offers a solution to these. In these apparitions we encounter a woman who remains ever close, warm and motherly, and yet exudes a power and presence that engenders faith and hope. From the first violent beginnings of the faith in the Americas to the everyday life in a contemporary communist state, Mary remains the universal mother who is able to be completely and significantly of the time and place. She is as much mother to us, Christ's disciples today, as she was to the beloved disciple when her Son said his "Behold your son." He says to each one of us now: Behold your mother, the woman revealed by the Scriptures and the Tradition and who gives warmth to that revelation by continuing apparitions.

BIBLIOGRAPHICAL NOTE

In this chapter I have made no attempt to treat of the apparitions of Mary in a complete fashion. I have sought only to bring forth elements which I felt could help us to understand and appreciate Mary more. The apparitions, though, are important as well as fascinating and you might want to pursue further reading in regard to them. For that reason I offer here a brief selective list of books that you might find helpful.

Guadalupe (1531)

Cassidy, Joseph, *Mexico, Land of Mary's Wonders*, Paterson, N.J.: St. Anthony Guild, 1958.

Leies, Herbert, *Mother for a New World, Our Lady of Guadalupe*, Westminster, Md.: The Newman Press, 1964.

Smith, Jody, *The Image of Guadalupe*, Garden City, N.Y.: Doubleday, 1983.

Paris (1830)

Englebert, Omer, *Catherine Labouré and the Modern Apparitions of Our Lady*, New York: Kennedy, 1959.

Dirvin, Joseph, *St. Catherine Labouré of the Miraculous Medal*, New York: Farrar, Straus and Cudahy, 1958.

La Salette (1846)

Kennedy, John, *Light on the Mountain, The Story of La Salette*, Garden City, N.Y.: Doubleday, 1956.

O'Reilly, James, *The Story of La Salette*, Chicago: Paluch, 1953.

Lourdes (1858)

Klein, James, *Thunder in the Valley*, Boston: St. Paul Editions, 1981.

Laurentin, René, *Bernadette of Lourdes: A Life Based on Authenticated Documents*, Minneapolis: Winston Press, 1979.

Marnham, Patrick, *Lourdes: A Modern Pilgrimage*, Garden City, N.Y.: Doubleday, 1982.

St.-Pierre, Michael, *Bernadette and Lourdes*, Garden City, N.Y.: Doubleday, 1955.

Knock (1879)

Rynne, Catherine, *Knock, 1879–1979*, Dublin: Veritas, 1979.

Fatima (1917)

Brochado, Costa, *Fatima in the Light of History,* Milwaukee: Bruce, 1955.

Fox, Robert, *Rediscovering Fátima,* Huntington, Ind.: Our Sunday Visitor, 1982.

Kondon, Louis, ed., *Fatima in Lucia's Own Words: Sister Lucia's Memoirs,* Fátima, Portugal: Postulation Centre, 1976.

Pelletier, Joseph, *The Sun Danced at Fatima,* Worcester, Mass.: Assumption Publications, 1951.

Walsh, William, *Our Lady of Fatima,* Garden City, N.Y.: Doubleday, 1947.

Beauraing (1932–33)

Amatora, Mary, *The Queen's Heart of Gold: The Complete Story of Our Lady of Beauraing,* New York: Pageant Press, 1957.

Sharkey, Don, and Debergh, Joseph, *Our Lady of Beauraing,* St. Meinrad, Ind.: Abbey Press, 1973.

Banneux (1933)

Beevers, John, *Virgin of the Poor: The Apparitions of Our Lady of Banneux,* St. Meinrad, Ind.: Abbey Press, 1972.

Medjugorje (1981—)

Kraljevic, Svetozar, *The Apparitions of Our Lady at Medjugorje, 1981–1983,* Chicago: Franciscan Herald Press, 1984.

Laurentin, René, and Rupeic, Ljudevit, *Is the Virgin Mary Appearing at Medjugorje?,* Washington, D.C.: The Word Among Us Press, 1984.

General

Connorm, Edward, *Recent Apparitions of Our Lady,* Fresno, Calif.: Academy Guild Press, 1960.

Delaney, John, ed., *A Woman Clothed with the Sun,* Garden City, N.Y.: Doubleday, 1971.

Odell, Catherine M., *Those Who Saw Her,* Huntington, Ind.: Our Sunday Visitor, 1986.

Further Reflections

We have listened to the Scriptures, to some of the voices of Tradition, most notably the two thousand bishops gathered at the Second Vatican Council, and to Mary herself, who has continued to speak to us in word and deed through her many apparitions on earth. In the course of our listening, we have shared some reflections. As I indicated in the introduction, looking at one facet and then at another, of this wondrous expression of God's beauty and love that is the virgin mother of his Son, I do not hope to draw it all together. There is so much more; in a sense, infinitely more, for Mary, like each of us, is created in the image and likeness of God. It is the joy of all our relationships that there is ever more to discover of the beauty of each other. There is always more to be discovered in regard to this beautiful person who is Mary. In this chapter I would just like to share a few more reflections that have emerged from my experience of Mary.

One day it dawned on me that there is another wholly different way of seeing things, a truer way: to see things as God sees them, in his eternal "now." I must confess when I first received this insight I was a bit put out with our God. There he was, resting in his glory, fully enjoying the finished product: St. Basil. And here I was, struggling along, far, far from that blissful consummation. Then I thought of Matt Talbot, lying eighteen years in the gutter, dead drunk. Things haven't been that bad—yet! The Lord has his ways with each of us. He allows us to exercise our freedom even in stupid adolescent ways. But the embrace of his love never lets go. We are always loved in his eternal love. The truer reality is that which exists ever in him—the finished product.

This is preeminently true of Mary. It is the holy and glorious, assumed virgin Queen, mother of God himself, enthroned at the side of his ascended Son, who is the reality—Mary. Yet, as with ourselves, there is the other side of the reality: the holy woman in the making, who walked our pilgrim ways. It is this Mary whom it can probably be more helpful for us to know and contemplate as we continue on our pilgrimage. The finished product, the realized fullness of divinized humanity, the woman assumed into heaven and glorified, is for us a constant sign and cause of hope. We do not want to lose sight of her or forget that she is the same woman who did live a very ordinary human life in a little town called Nazareth, who didn't understand everything, even though her Son was God, living right with her, praying and reading the Scriptures with her. She had her questions and her fears. Our daily stumbling and bumbling does not separate us from our ultimate fulfillment and glorification. (Do you feel uncomfortable, as I do, in thinking about and speaking about your own glorification? We have been so schooled in adopting a hangdog humility before God that it is difficult for us to break free and really sing our own *Magnificat*. We are destined to be glorious! The alternative is unthinkable.) In God's mysterious design—"Your thoughts are not my thoughts, nor my ways your ways, says the Lord"—his is the way, the only way, to get there.

So we do want to see Mary as a fellow traveler, and thus one who can inspire, enlighten and encourage us on the way. At the same time, we do want to see Mary in all her glory, in order to know her as we ought—and in that to glorify her Son, the Source and Cause of all her glory—and to let her be for us a source of hope.

Mary is a woman of both time and eternity, as we all are. We accept her as portrayed in our basic source, the Gospels, with her perplexities and anxieties, her intellectual limitations. She may well have had her moments of enlightenment, most certainly she did— anyone who prays seriously and searches the Scriptures regularly does. But we have no basis on which to say much about this dimension of Mary's consciousness, only some conjectures, with varying degrees of probability.

But Mary is not only an historical personage. She is that, and in being that, being the particular historical person who she is, she is also a symbol, a symbol of faith, an expression of the Divine Love, a theological reality. There is here place for that development of doctrine of which we have previously spoken.

We see some development already taking place in the sacred,

inspired Scriptures. The earliest Scripture reference to Mary, wholly in the context of Christ, as are all the writings of the New Testament, simply states her fundamental role, that of the woman who gave birth to Jesus: "born of a woman." So St. Paul. Mark the evangelist seems to notice Mary only as being one among the rest of Jesus' relatives, not really distinguishing her from the rest. Reflection continued to go on within the Christian community. When Matthew and Luke came to write their Gospel narratives, there was more to be said. Matthew saw Mary in her role of fulfilling the prophecies: a virgin shall conceive and bear a son. Luke goes further and sets her forth as the woman of faith, the one who hears the Word of God and keeps it. This faithful hearing is the source of her maternity and makes her a true disciple. Finally, it is John, the last of the New Testament writers, who introduces the theology of the Woman, showing Mary's role of mothering, modeling and mediation. He points to ultimate eschatological fulfillment in his Book of Revelations.

Development continued, especially as the Good News of Jesus Christ came to peoples of other cultures. They reflected on Jesus and his mother and her role in his Church. Such development can and should go on in our times and in all future times. The "symbol" of Mary can be enriched still further by the use of the symbols of cultures other than those which have been dominant in our Christian thinking up to now. Mary herself, in the ways she has appeared and the places she has appeared, invites this.

The Blessed Virgin's appearance on Tepeyac is perhaps one of the better illustrations of this. There she comes as an Aztec maiden, apparently pregnant, one with a people and culture which was being invited to bring forth a new church. She came to these people not as someone apart and foreign, not as one identified with the dominating, albeit catholic, force and culture. She came as one of their women, clothed as they would be clothed, adorned not only with the cross of her Son but also with the symbols sacred to their nation and culture. She came to a place sacred to their goddess, a goddess of fertility, inviting all the symbolism that surrounded that goddess to be brought over—as it were baptized, just as early Christians baptized feasts and festivals, signs and symbols, of the pagan Roman religion—and converted to find its place within a true, enriched understanding and experience of Mary and of her Son.

In doing this Mary invited countless millions into the Church, into understanding and acceptance of her Son Jesus as Lord and Savior, that Son hidden within her.

In this kind of development a lot of careful sifting needs to be done. It is something that cannot be done adequately by persons outside the culture. This is why the breakthrough of the Second Vatican Council, empowering the collegiality of the hierarchy and recognizing the important role of national and regional conferences of bishops, is so essential for the ongoing development of doctrine. The scholastically trained westerners in Rome cannot hope to discern adequately whether or not an interpretation of the Revelation expressed in the light of Vedic philosophy is completely consonant with true Christian faith. It is for the bishops of India who are steeped in their own traditional culture and its philosophy to make such discernment under the Holy Spirit. This is equally true in regard to the use of Zen philosophy in Japan, which engenders most extraordinary and profoundly beautiful insights into the interpretation of the Gospels—insights of which we of the West, especially those of us who have had some Zen experience under a good master, can catch some glimpses, yet most of which elude us because of their rootedness in another cultural experience.

This has certainly been my experience sitting at the feet of Father Oshida. This Japanese Dominican's story is a most interesting one. He grew up a Buddhist and received the Christian faith only in his late teens. Soon after, he entered the Dominican order. Studying for the priesthood he regularly got terrible headaches trying to understand and absorb scholastic theology. For relief he began sitting Zen, something he had not done as a practice when he was a Buddhist. His great breakthrough came when he studied Hebrew. Then, for the first time, he heard the Scriptures, the original Hebrew Scriptures and the Greek Scriptures, in the light of the Hebrew, as a Japanese, rather than filtering everything through Greco-Roman philosophical thought patterns and languages. It was a marvelous revelation for him. When Father Oshida gives a teisho, a homily or commentary on the Scriptures, there is little that I grasp, but the few shafts of light that I do get are immensely illuminating for they come from a totally different direction than the one I am used to in receiving the Revelation. Father has not yet offered us anything on Mary, but I am eagerly awaiting the time when he does.

Just as the profound beauty of the Christian Revelation that has been brought forth to us by the Greco-Roman culture and philosophy has been almost inaccessible to Asiatics and Africans (with the result that Christianity presented in European garb has found few among the millions able to embrace it), so we of the West need humbly to accept that our brothers and sisters of other cultures are able to find beauty and insight in the Revelation which we will hardly be able to share. But we can each and all bring the fullness of our gift to the whole, allowing the Church, Bride of Christ, his People come together, to show forth an incomprehensible beauty for his delight and glory.

* * *

In emphasizing the importance for us to be in touch with Mary, the fellow pilgrim, the woman growing in understanding, I do not want in any way to deny the reality and the importance of any of Mary's special graces and prerogatives. It is a question of both/and, not either/or. The thinking that has guided much of the theological development concerning Mary, leading us to magnify her greatness —in accord with her own *Magnificat*—may not be as wide of the mark as some would have us think.

Jesus appealed to the basic instincts which have been planted in us by God our Creator as a means to help us know and understand how God acts in our regard: Which of you, if your child asks for bread, will give him a stone? If he asks for a fish, will give him a snake? If you who are evil know how to give good things to your children, how much more so will your Father in heaven give good things to those who ask him? Then: Which of you, if you could, would not keep your mother safe from all sin and the domination of the evil one? Which of you, if you could, would not preserve from corruption that body from which you were formed and drew life and nurture? Who of you does not honor his mother all he can? If you who are evil would do these things for your mother, how much more so would not I, the perfect Son, do this for the Woman from whom I received the gift of human life, love and caring—my mother?

The old scholastic dictum was *Potuit, decuit, fecit*—he could do it, it was fitting, therefore he did it. Everything that was fitting for Jesus to do in regard to his mother, he did. I don't think anyone would argue against that. If there are disagreements, it is precisely in the area of what we think is fitting for Jesus to do for his mother.

There are many things that will color our judgment here. Mary, in the earliest time, was seen primarily from a Christological viewpoint, wholly in relation to Jesus the Christ. This is undoubtedly the most important and most basic insight. More recently there developed a mariology, a study of Mary in herself. Here exaggeration has been more apt to creep in. With the most recent renewal, Mary is seen more in an ecclesiological context, as one of the pilgrim people of God. This perspective will help to bring any previous exaggerations into balance, but it should not negate anything that is true in them.

* * *

Discourse about God *(theo-logia)* and the things of God (including Mary) and the relationship of God to humankind is determined by human experience in time and space. Theology always interacts with the contemporary anthropology, which is ever in evolution. Therefore, it is socioculturally conditioned. I am a United States American, thinking and writing in the final days of the twentieth century. All of this colors all that I think and say and write. In addition, each of us is the product of our background, our studies, of those who have formed and influenced us. Because of this we are apt to see things somewhat differently, in ways that are complementary and mutually enriching, I hope.

Differences, disagreement and even contradictions are not in themselves bad. Have you ever visited the study hall of a yeshiva? For those of us who are used to the largely silent decorum of our normal high school or college study hall, it is a shock. The place seems to be in absolute chaos. Everywhere, on all sides, students are shouting at each other, usually gesticulating wildly. The students have been paired off and are arguing opposite sides of the questions they are studying. Their whole being enters into this process of learning, making it one that will leave a lasting impression. Arguments are marshaled with great energy. There is no lack of interest here, there are no sleeping students. In the course of the intense controversy, new insights burst forth and lessons are easily remembered. This is much the way Jesus taught. He countered questions with questions and arguments with arguments. Arguments, as buttresses and arches, put pressure on one another to support the whole. Opinions press against each other until new insight comes forth.

The development of the doctrine of the immaculate conception of Mary is a good example of this. The question arose early and through the centuries saints stood firmly on both sides. The universal role of Christ as savior did not seem to allow for a sinless Mary before the redemption. Yet the thought that Mary was even for the least moment under the domination of the evil one was too abhorrent to accept, considering her intimate role in the incarnation. Finally, there burst forth the insight. Given the presence of all times in the now of God, there is no reason why God could not apply the fruit of Christ's redemption prior to its actual happening in time. Indeed, this is what brought salvation to all those who lived in justice before the historical coming of Christ. It seems an obvious solution once we hear it, but it took centuries for it to come forth.

I am reminded of a story about Christopher Columbus, back in Spain for the celebrations after his successful first voyage to the Americas. One of the guests at his table rather demeaned his accomplishment. After all, it was just a matter of sailing west. Columbus quietly took an egg and invited the men at the table to stand it on its end. The egg passed from hand to hand, each guest making his fumbling attempts, but the egg never quite stayed erect. When the egg arrived back in the hands of Columbus, he reached for the salt dish and easily stood the egg on its end in the salt. All had a good laugh and Columbus made his point. Once the insight is had, everyone can easily stand an egg on its end.

Prior to the moment of enlightenment, things just didn't come together. Once the insight is gained, everything seems so facile and clear. Oftentimes such precious insights come out of controversy. So we need not fear being in disagreement. We will profit by it if we allow each other's experience and contribution to challenge us to re-examine our own positions.

*   *   *

Let us now look at some of the facets of this incomprehensible mystery we call Mary.

THE IMMACULATE CONCEPTION

Reviewing the apparitions of Mary in the last century I was struck by how often the mystery of Mary's immaculate conception came to the fore. It was the century within which the development of this doctrinal insight, which was had some centuries before, came to fullness and was solemnly set forth by the Church. The same grace that was being given us through the teaching authority within the Church was being given to the life and practice of the faithful directly by Mary through her several apparitions. At Paris the grace came forth in the form of a medal with a prayer to be said: O Mary, conceived without sin, pray for us who have recourse to you. At Lourdes it was the name Mary gave herself as the source of the healing that is to be found there: I am the Immaculate Conception. In our century, at Fátima, Mary began to center on the symbol of the heart and so she spoke of and showed her immaculate heart. At Beauraing, the woman who called herself the Immaculate showed her heart, that glistened as if it were of gold.

This fuller development of the doctrine of the immaculate conception seems to have been saved for our times. Why?

I believe this is so because it responds to concerns which have arisen with our development of psychological insight. Perhaps, also, it has something to do with the development that is taking place in regard to our understanding of just what original sin is and how it operates within us. In recent years we have become more and more acutely aware of how past experiences, which have become lodged within us in the form of memories, color and even dominate the way we function and respond to life. Thus great emphasis has come to be laid on the healing of memories, exorcising these demons of the past so that we may meet today with openness and freedom and receive today's grace in its fullness. With the development of psychological insight as well as the physiological sciences, we have come to realize that this storehouse of memories which so conditions us begins to be filled very early, in fact it would seem from the very first moment of our conception, and even prior to conception in so far as the egg and sperm that come together carry their own histories. Thus our need for healing, in order to find true freedom and complete openness to our full personal development, goes back to the moment we are conceived and come into being. The inherited binding that comes to us through ovum and sperm is something of the fabric of original sin.

The realization that Christ's grace reached so deeply into Mary that it healed her totally from the very first moment of her conception, so that all the binding that she should have normally inherited was never experienced by her, bears powerful witness to us to what we can hope for from that same redeeming grace of Christ. Mary's complete healing assures us that we can be completely healed if we but open ourselves ever more fully to the grace of Christ. Mary, a fully human person, one of the redeemed, is like us in all things but sin. Her freedom from sin is promise and pledge of that to which we can aspire. No matter how deep-rooted the tendencies toward disintegration, self-hate and darkness are in us, no matter how surely they are programmed in our genes, we have a witness that the grace of Christ can indeed reach to them and wholly heal them, giving us that fullness of freedom for which we long.

Even as the immaculate conception glorifies the grace and power of Christ's redemption and honors the recipient of that grace, his mother, this is a personal message it has for us, a message which only in our times at our point in evolution are we ready to receive. This is perhaps one of the reasons why this particular development of doctrine has come to fullness in our times.

The immaculate conception also proclaims to us another message, that of true freedom. The immaculate conception stands for freedom, perfect freedom, freedom from the domination of sin and passion. The freedom to be wholly to God, to be all we are meant to be. Aptly was Mary under the title of the Immaculate Conception chosen as the patroness of this land dedicated to freedom. We need constantly to look to Mary to understand what is true freedom, to distinguish it from license. Mary's freedom from sin and passion gave her the freedom to serve and suffer, to be a complete yes to God. I fear too few United States Americans see their freedom in this way. It is the way, the only way, to true dignity and power. It is the only way to human and Christian fulfillment.

Mary Mediatrix

Mary has certainly exercised an absolutely unique mediation between God and the human family, as one of that human family.

A mediator is someone who is able to stand between two groups or at least has a special in with both sides so that she or he can hope to bring the two sides together. Mary, because of the foreseen merits of her Son, was in the first moment of her existence totally graced and pleasing to God. Although she was completely one with us in our humanity, she stood out in a special way from our humanity in this gracefulness. So it was that God, when he wanted to become one with us by embracing as his own our humanity, turned to Mary. God had every right to claim humanity as his own. Yet as the Creator he has always been more profoundly reverent of his creation than anyone else. He knows that the greatest thing that he has given to the human person is our freedom because therein lies our power to love, to be like God, for God is love. When God wanted to partake of our humanity, he looked for a free yes from us. It was Mary who stood there in our name and said that yes. The medieval fantasy of a man like Bernard of Clairvaux, who depicts the whole human race gathered around Mary encouraging her to say that yes, waiting with bated breath until she does say it, is not altogether fanciful.

As I have mentioned before, we tend to think of things in our dimension of passing time. One thing follows after the other and is separated from the other by the lapse of time. But that is not the way things really are in God's eternal now. All is. Everything is existent in God's now as one. When Mary stood before God and said her yes, each and every one of us was there. When we, in spirit, unite our yes with Mary's, it becomes integrated with the yes of humanity that Mary is saying. Mary was our mediatrix, our spokesperson before the Divine. She was the one who, by God's own doing, was the human person so graced that she was more worthy than any of us to say that yes and was able to say that yes more freely and totally than any of us who are divided by our sin and passion. Thus Mary, in a very real and special sense, is our mediatrix.

Does her mediation stop there? No, by no means. And neither does ours.

When God did become man and the Son of God embraced our humanity, then indeed we had *the* mediator—one who belonged totally to both sides and brought them together in deepest harmony and union. It was this mediator's yes to the Father that truly reconciled humanity with the divine and made it possible to offer us all the grace to be divinized. He merited the grace and graciousness that Mary had in order to be able to fill her role of mediation at the incarnation and also at Calvary and beyond.

We sometimes seem to have an almost materialistic idea of grace. As though it were something that was poured into us, distributed or meted out. That is not what we are talking about at all. Grace is the inflow of the divine action, life and love in us, making us more and more integral, more and more like unto God, more and more fully partakers of his divine life, nature and being. It is Jesus' total and complete yes, with all the fullness of God expressed from a human heart, that opened the way for the totality of the divine life and love to flow into the human race. At the moment that he expressed that yes in its fullness on Calvary's hill, the one chosen by God to stand at his side and be a total yes with his yes was Mary, his mother: There stood by the cross of Jesus his mother.

Again, the reality that all time is one in God's now comes into play here. Each and every one of us, most especially at the moment when that sacrament of Calvary is made present in our midst in the holy sacrifice of the mass, but at any time, can say our yes with the yes of Jesus and Mary. In that moment the divine life and love flows into us and through us into the rest of the human family. The union we have with one another as members of the one body of Christ, the union we have in the solidarity of our humanity, is such that when-ever any one of us says yes and receives into his being the inflowing of divine life and love, it flows in some way into the entire body, into the entire human family. Jesus, the mediator, was the only one who could say an adequate yes to God, big enough for the divine life and love in all its fullness. Mary's yes, because of her sinlessness, be-cause of her intimate union with Christ, was as complete as would be possible for any human person. In that sense she received a fullness of grace from Christ, beyond which no one else ever has. And each of us, to the extent to which we say yes, that we are integrated, that we are open, that we are completely a yes to God, do we receive his grace and life, and through us so do others. To that extent we are all mediators. Christ's mediation is infinitely beyond Mary's and that of the rest of us because the person who says yes is God. Mary's mediation is essentially the same as ours. But we can believe that hers has a fullness and openness and a oneness with Christ's that it is possible for all his fullness to pour into her and through her to the rest of us in her universal care and concern.

Again, in our materialistic outlook we tend to think of creation as something which God sat down one day and put together and set on its own, all finished. That is not a true, adequate understanding of what is going on. God did not make us out of something. Nor did he make us out of nothing.

Remember that scene in the Gospels when the rich young man ran up to Jesus and said: Good Master, what must I do to have eternal life? Jesus, being a good Jew, a good rabbi, answered the question with a question: Why do you call me good? One is good, God. Jesus, of course, was inviting the young man to say: But you are God. The young man was not ready for that. However, Jesus, in that statement, was also making a statement about reality, which we might call an ontological or metaphysical statement. One is: God; one is good: God. And everything else that is, that has goodness, has being and goodness only to the extent to which it participates in the being and goodness of God. God does not make us out of nothing. God shares with us something of his own being and goodness and beauty. And he does that at every moment, from moment to moment. Our creator is never away from us, leaving us as a job that is finished. At every moment he is bringing us forth, sharing his being, his life, his goodness with us.

God has so ordained and decided that the way that he is going to bring forth and form the creation in the next moment, the next hour, the next day, or the next week is to some extent going to be decided by us. Thus he says: ask and you shall receive. According as we ask, so it is done.

There is a fittingness here, because in so far as we are yes to God, divine grace flows into us and through us into the creation. God, reverencing our freedom, the freedom he has given us, allows us to decide to some extent the way in which that life, that love, that created power of God, which is called grace, flows into us, and through us into our fellow human beings and into this whole creation.

In this sense, then, we are all mediators of grace. Mary, because of the completeness of her yes and the intimacy of her union with Christ, we can indeed believe, is the mediatrix of all grace. All the grace that flows from God, all the life and love and mercy that flows from God, comes through Jesus Christ; we know that. God wills also that it flows from Christ to Mary and through Mary to the rest of us. This is what we mean by the mediation of Mary, that Mary is the mediatrix of all graces. In the fullness of her yes, in her mediation she obtains for us the grace which allows us to be mediators, to be women and men who say a complete yes to God and receive the fullness of divine life and grace and love into ourselves and into all those for whom we have a caring love.

In this we can, again, see Mary as the first of the disciples, not only in time—at the annunciation and the incarnation—but in pre-eminence, by virtue of the way she heard the word of God and said a complete yes to it by the grace she received from God because of the merits of her Son. Thus she models for each of us the way to be true disciples, to say yes to God, accepting him into our humanity, and saying yes to God in that supreme act of love that is Calvary.

We know that Jesus longed to fulfill the will of his Father, to become that complete yes that Calvary is. Greater love than this no man has than he lay down his life. He longed to give this fullest expression of obedience and love to his father. And yet he was human. We know that he sweat blood and cried to his Father: If it be possible, let this chalice pass. When Mary stood by him at the cross, she said again her *fiat*, the yes to God that she said at the annunciation; she said it fully and totally. And yet in her mother's heart she shared all the anguish that her Son experienced. There is a deep part of her that said: Father, why must this be done? So, in our own lives. Even as we, at the bottom line, say yes to God, we can experience a lot of pull in other directions, a lot of anguish, a lot of questioning: Why, God? Why this way? St. Paul spoke about a law in his members that fought against his spirit. We know that we have experienced that. It doesn't detract anything from our yes, if we do not let it. Jesus' cry—Father, if it be possible . . .—didn't take anything away from his complete yes. Mary's motherly anguish didn't take anything away from her complete yes. And so our own troubled spirit does not need to take anything away from our yes and our being wide open to receiving the divine love and creative activity called grace not only for ourselves but for the whole human family.

In our struggle to be a complete yes to God, we can again look to Mary, the mediatrix of all graces, as model, as source, as companion and fellow disciple.

The Virgin Wife

One of the aspects of Mary's virginity, one often missed in the Church in the past because of the tendency to look upon all women as Eve, the seducer of men, is that virginity, consecrated and made fruitful by the Lord, does not exclude close, even intimate relations with someone of the other sex.

Mary, virgin of virgins, was bonded to Joseph in the closest and most intimate of human relations. She was, in law and in fact, by divine providence, the wife of Joseph the carpenter. She lived all her life, from the blossoming of her maidenhood till death separated them, in closest daily proximity and life sharing with him.

Perhaps only in a situation where the God to whom we commit

ourselves in embracing virginity or celibacy for the kingdom is the Child in whom the couple's love is centered, is it possible for virginity and marital love to be so fully present in one couple. Most of us suffer from the more human effect which St. Paul speaks about when he says that the heart of the married is divided. Most of us need space to live a love totally dedicated to God. But none of us can be complete or move toward total integration in a virginity that excludes, fears and is closed to warm human relations.

Mary's total being to God in virginity was in every way supported and accompanied by her husband's love and care and her love and care for him was totally within this love for God, their Child. There is a coming together here that we can all strive for and emulate as we seek to "mother" the Christ in ourselves and in our intimate friends —the one same Christ in us all.

Mary gives witness to the married that the fullness of virginal love of God is not necessarily outside their married love if the couple center together on forming Christ in themselves, in each other, and in their children—the one same Christ in all.

Mary was able to accept the collaboration of a man in a most intimate way, as was required by the needs of the vocation that was hers as a virgin mother. Each of them, Mary and Joseph, accepted their respective vocations in regard to God's salvific plan which called for a very intimate relationship between them, and yet each retained that uniquely free stance of a virginal heart before God and in their relationship. It is in this sense that virginity has its place in every marriage. It is in this primary being, being a yes to God, that the partners come together as equals and bring each their proper gift to the relationship, with a profound respect for the uniqueness of the other and that to which God is calling the other. There is no effort on the part of either to dominate the other, no desire to make the other conform to one's own ideal. Both wife and husband, standing in the power of that freedom that comes from being primarily to God, have the freedom to be totally to each other in marital love, a free and complete gift, bringing something of the infinite richness and beauty of a love sourced in the divine, a love which can constantly call the other forth and totally satisfy the other by the fullness of its potential and realization.

WOMAN OF PRAYER

"Mary pondered all these things in her heart."

Again and again St. Luke tells us this of Mary. It is repeated because it is the basic stance of this woman of God. It is a basically feminine way to respond to the challenges and mysteries of life. To be still and be with.

In order to be integral, in order to be whole, men need this feminine dimension as much as women.

This "pondering" of which St. Luke speaks is not the same as thinking. I was dismayed when I found that one of the newer English translations of the Scriptures so translated the text. Mary did not just think these things over. Thinking is still something very active, dominating, very much the male thing: pull it apart and master it. What our poor little minds can master will not take us beyond ourselves. There will be no ecstasy, no new creation.

"Ponder" means to let the reality weigh in our hearts. Let it be there. Let it be felt. Let it make its impression. Note, it is in the heart, not the mind. It begins in the mind, that is where we learn of the reality. But, as the Byzantine Christians put it, the mind must come down into the heart.

It is the fourfold process of the traditional *lectio: lectio,* receiving the reality that is revelatory of God; *meditatio,* letting it quietly be present, perhaps repeating the expressive word, until it forms the heart and calls forth a response from within us: *oratio,* prayer. When the reality completely reveals itself to us as being of the divine goodness and beauty, then our response can only be total: *contemplatio,* contemplation. We are one with it.

Mary let the things that were beyond her, that she did not understand, be there in her heart. She did not reject them or argue with them; she was humble enough to be subject to them. She let them be with her till they expanded and formed her heart to that love and understanding that was consonant with and supported her complete yes to God.

Mary, even as she went about the details of her everyday life as mother and housewife was a contemplative. She let things speak to her, not only superficially, but deeply. Deep calls unto deep. The deep reality of each of them, the ground where they were coming forth from God's creative love, spoke to the depths of her own being, spoke to her of God. She quietly received that revelation into her depths and let it call her forth in the complete harmony of a yes, the perfect yes of love. At the same time she allowed the deep mysteries that had been revealed to her, that were taking place in her own life as she bore, nurtured and educated God's son, rest in her, not wholly understood. They did not need to be wholly understood. Rather she let them form a heart in her that would be able continuously to say a complete yes and to move steadily with her Son to that consummation of her original yes which would take place on Calvary's hill. A quiet openness to reality enabled her to still be the yes of complete faith in the blackness and emptiness of Holy Saturday, wide open to receive in its fullness the joy of Easter and the powerful new outpouring of the Spirit at Pentecost. Mary didn't need answers, hers was the open space of the question, wide open to whatever the Divine would have. Hers was an openness and a yes to God big enough to allow him to become incarnate within her. The restrictions of human thought and mastery could never be open enough for that.

From Mary we all need to learn how to ponder in the heart.

Pondering was Mary's essential and constant prayer. As a young Jew she searched the Scriptures—at home, for only men were allowed to do it in the synagogue—and entered more and more deeply into the longings of her faithful people. These longings perhaps became fullest when they were already being fulfilled, as Mary longed for the coming forth of the Child that lived within her. Only one who has been a pregnant mother can fully enter into such longing and expectation.

In response to her longings, God had revealed himself as never before. To Mary, at the moment of the annunciation, came the first revelation of the inner triune personality of God. How much she understood at that moment we have no way of telling. Some comprehension was necessary for her to respond to his request in a way that is consonant with human freedom and dignity. The enlightenment of grace that enables any one of us to accept the mystery of the Trinity would certainly have been given to her. The experience of God the Father and Jesus the Son and the Holy Spirit that gradually becomes ours through prayer could only have had a beginning in this first moment of revelation. In any case, Mary did say yes to the Father and received his Son as hers by the overshadowing of Holy Spirit. It was a moment of revelation that profoundly transformed her prayer. She would bow her head in reverence to the God of her fathers who dwelt in his holy temple in the heavens and in Jerusalem and know that he also dwelt in her as Son.

There is no wonder then that what record we have of Mary's prayer is marked with praise. Pondering deeply the mystery being worked in her, she could not but burst forth in praise, especially when she came upon someone who could, in some deeper way, share her experience. Mary in her *Magnificat* fittingly summed up all the praise of God of her people. For what God had always done for his people he had now done preeminently for Mary. He had, indeed, exalted the humble. This lowest daughter of the family of David, living in Nazareth, symbolic of the depths to which the royal family, the family of promise, had fallen, was to be the queen mother of David's heir, the heir who would reign forever. Essential to a prayer of praise is that true humility, the humility of truth, that knows our lowliness and at the same time can proclaim our magnificence, for he that is mighty has done great things for us—all of us, in Mary and in our own creation and re-creation in Christ.

Mary is a model for us, too, in the prayer of petition. As a mother I suppose she often asked Jesus to do little things around the house. In a sense he got used to doing what she wanted. His one recorded adolescent escapade concludes with the statement that he returned home and was subject to her and Joseph. As with all women and men, there came a time when there was a shift in the relationship between parent and child. We, as it were, see that shift in progress at Cana. In that incident Mary shows us how to approach her Son with our needs.

Mary, in fact, makes no demand on Jesus at Cana. She doesn't even suggest to her Son how he should respond to the need that has arisen. With unshakable faith, a faith that can withstand even an apparent deaf ear or denial, she places the need before her Son. It is a need that comes from the heart, the caring heart of a mother—the kind of prayer I think the Lord most likes to hear. In every case, he does not listen to the words on the lips, he listens to the heart. It is heartfelt concern to which he responds. Heartfelt concern that knows he will take care of things, and moves ahead in that confidence, doing whatever he tells us, knowing that in that is to be found the fulfillment of all our prayer.

The last time the Scriptures reveal the mother of Jesus to us she is in prayer in the midst of the Church. Our prayer needs always to come from within the Church. It is only within the Church, within the body of Christ, that we are alive and can offer a living prayer.

Mary remains where the Scriptures have left her, within the Church praying. Mary is with us always within the body of Christ. Mary continues to be with all Christians in their prayer. And so our prayer becomes effective, for whenever two agree on anything the Lord is ready to respond. So he has said. Mary exercises her mediation in our prayer, not so much as one handing it on for us, but as one who is at our side praying with us, making our prayer her own, bringing to it the purity and detachment of her immaculate heart. And she clearly indicates to us the way to be most sure of the fulfillment of our prayer—which, incidentally, will all too often take a form quite different from what we expect: My ways are not your ways . . . When we have prayed, have confidently placed our need before the Lord, then we are to do whatever he tells us.

MARY AND THE CHURCH

Mother of the Church is a very ancient title of Mary. We find its implications richly developed among the fathers and mothers as well as among some of the theologians of our own times, such as that present-day father of the Church, Henri Cardinal de Lubac. It is, as we have seen, a title solidly based on the theology found in the Gospel of St. John and in the Book of Revelations. It is present by implication in the other Gospel narratives.

Isaac of Stella, one of the deeper theologians of the twelfth century, tells us that what is true of the Church as a whole is preeminently true of Mary and is true of each soul individually. This thought is not far from that of Jewish mysticism which sees the same sort of relationship between Israel as the Bride of Yahweh and the individual faithful Jew. It is also solidly rooted in Christian tradition.

In considering Mary in relation to the Church we have to be careful of two possible extremes: One, which is perhaps the greater danger today, would be to so immerse Mary within the People of God, the community of the faithful, that we lose sight of her unique role in the Church. This has been the failing of some of the Christian churches. It results in failing to understand the Church and its mission in its fullness and keeps us from appreciating the role Mary can play in our lives as Christians. The opposite danger, to which catholics were more prone before the Second Vatican Council, is to separate Mary too much from the rest of the pilgrim people of God, which is contrary to the divine plan and the reality. There is only one Body of Christ. Mary is a part of it, just as we are.

We understand the Church better when we understand Mary better. And we understand Mary better when we understand the Church better. Both have maternal roles in regard to individual members of the Body of Christ. Neither can be separated from the members. We are the Church and Mary is one with us in being the Church, the Body of Christ.

Mary, in fact, anteceded the Church and was instrumental in its coming into being by her yes at the annunciation. Her yes was essentially the yes of humanity, of our human family, to becoming God's People in a new way—that way being the Church. All our yesses are, as it were, contained in her yes and find a fullness in hers. And her yes is possible because of Christ's and finds its fullness— even as does ours—in the yes of Christ, the Son to the Father. Our yes is one with Mary's in Christ's. As Christ came to do the will of the Father, he called forth Mary's yes and ours in hers. When I say yes to God today in writing this book or in fulfilling any of the other things the Lord asks of me, I say my yes with Christ and by his grace, and with Mary by the grace of Christ that comes to me through her yes. Here is the reality that is at the heart of the Church, that creates the Church in its oneness. Here is where we People are intimately one with Christ, with Mary, and with each other. One grace making possible all yesses as one yes.

As a result of her yes at the annunciation, Mary welcomed God within her in a most special way. She formed him, giving him a human body, and not just a body but a full humanity. However, Christ came and assumed a body, assumed human nature, not just to be one man but to unite all humans to himself, to have a mystical body. In our sequential time the formation and development of Christ's mystical body has followed the formation of his physical body in the womb of Mary, but in the divine design and reality the one did not take place apart from the other. As Mary formed and nurtured the Head, she exercised a maternal role in regard to the members. In the flow of time, this gestation still goes on. Mary is ever pregnant, ever mothering.

Taking the image from her reality, we speak of the Church itself as mothering its members corporately and individually, acting out of their fullness, forming and bringing forth new members. Mary ever remains the foremost member of the Church, playing her part in the birthing of every other member both in her unending ministry to the Head and in her ministry to each of us in the order of grace. Our union with Mary in the Church is very immediate, intimate and effective.

Queen of the Apostles

Queen is a title which many of us feel a bit uncomfortable with today. Maybe there is some inconsistency here, when we think of all the interest shown in the pomp and ceremony of the reigning family across the sea so manifest at the time of the royal weddings. Not everyone, of course, shared that interest. Some saw the displays as so much "bread and circus"—mostly without the bread—while an empire decays. There is tragedy in spending millions on such affairs while millions go to bed hungry at home and more millions starve to death in former colonies and dependencies.

We in the United States can hardly point the finger at our sisters and brothers across the seas. Recall the pageantry in New York for the lighting up of an old statue. It was a bit frightening to hear commentators refer to the venerable statue as "Our Lady." Civil religion has come so far that our instinctual needs enthrone a feminine presence at the side of Uncle Sam. And this was being perpetrated by some of those who have traditionally berated catholics for their veneration of the holy Mother of God.

Recently I joined a family at the bedside of their dying son, a man in his thirties. He was in agony, his head incredibly swollen with a brain tumor. Later, as I returned to the experience, how my heart was wrung. (The image is apt. I felt as though two great hands, like those of a hearty peasant, wrung all my innards as she might wring out her towels or her husband's tough overalls—only I felt in no wise tough.) I thought of how wrung was the being of his mother. As Mary stood at the cross, I dare say, she was so transfixed (Simeon's sword) by the experience of the moment she could give no thought to ought else. Yet later, when she returned to the experience, there would be such a longing that each one for whom her Son went through that ordeal would not fail to receive the full benefit of it that this alone would warrant her title of queen or first of the apostles—the apostolic ones. For heaven looks to the heart, not to the feet or the lips, although the heart would not be true if it did not move the lips and the feet along the appropriate course of action.

We do not know in fact what the Woman did after she took the beloved disciple as her own, save that on the morrow of her Son's ascending she was in the midst of the apostles as they prayed and received the all-empowering Spirit sent by her Son to send them forth.

Traditions of various worth have their various stories. Even far-away Athos boasts of Mary's providential visit. Ephesus claims her final home. Jerusalem venerates her place of dormition and her empty tomb. The only tradition most solemnly ratified by the centuries with endless fidelity is that in the end she did not rest on earth but, perfect follower, she followed her Son, body and soul, into the heavenly places, to sit with him on his throne just as he sits with his Father on his Father's throne. *Assumpta est Maria in coelum*—Mary was assumed, lifted up into heaven.

As we walk among the everyday things of Nazareth, we find every argument against any of the extraordinary attributions with which tradition or apocrypha have surrounded and clothed this housewife and mother. Yet, when we stand close by the cross on Calvary's hill and therefore close by her or quake with the enlivening Spirit of the Cenacle, we can readily believe anything is possible. For what she suffered for and with the Lord no reward, no consolation, can be too much. She who stood her ground on Calvary deserves to sit with him in heaven—and without delay. She who received the same Spirit as the Twelve on Pentecost cannot but be powerfully Spirit-filled, an apostolic spirit that drives the possessed to every corner of creation with apostolic love and zeal.

If the Spirit can inflame our disgustingly tepid hearts and give us the victory to sit with him on his throne, what must the Spirit have done enlivening the heart of this valiant mother? If Calvary and Cenacle can move us to apostolic zeal and appropriate action, what must they have done to the maternal and queenly heart that always lived the openness of *fiat*—be it done unto me according to your word and will.

Hail, First of the Apostles, Queen of us all.

COMPANION IN PAIN

If we take up our cross daily and follow Christ, if we stand by the side of the cross on Calvary, we stand by the side of Mary. And she walks and stands by our side. We can lean on her understanding and support and wisdom. Christians have much to suffer today, perhaps more than ever.

It is a new age of martyrs. The catholic world, led by the Pope, honors outstanding ones such as Archbishop Oscar Romero of San Salvador. There are many lesser known ones such as the American priest, Father Steve Rother, who was shot to death on the doorstep of his church in Guatemala. More vague is our knowledge of many others who are suffering and dying in fidelity to Christ. Perhaps we are suffering our own subtle or not so subtle persecutions at the hands of our own government or Church and even at the hands of friends as we seek to be true to our consciences in marital fidelity, business practices, war taxes, sanctuary and so many other, not always clear, ways, when we seek to stand with the Prince of Peace and the Son of Justice.

If we love the Church, we are pained today by the struggle going on within our community of faith. Sometimes even leaders, claiming to have the mind of Christ, seem to be concerned more about consolidating their position and power than about building up the unity of the body and its life-giving diversity. We see men and women whom we love virtually persecuted by their fellow Christians because they have dared to express the questions that are the making of a development of doctrine.

If we have the mind and heart of Christ which reaches out to all the human family, we are devastated by the widespread suffering and miseries that the media day after day lay upon our hearts. Knowing the incredible bounty of our heavenly Father it is tragic to see how the politics of food can leave millions suffering and dying, how the manipulations of the armament industries and the multinationals leave vast numbers in subhuman conditions. Our helplessness comes home to us. Quite often we can only stand with Mary at the cross and offer our pain with Christ with the hope that it will be redemptive and healing.

I think of the pain of truly Christian parents who have the agony of seeing their beloved children forsake the only way to happiness and fulfillment. They have done their best to pass on the faith and to bring their children up well but there comes a time when the peer pressure and the onslaughts of consumerism take over and their children are led into ways that endanger not only their health and life but even their eternal salvation. Oftentimes there is little that parents can do but watch and pray with Mary.

Akin to the painful concern that weighed so heavy on Mary's heart is that of the uncomprehending parents who see their children follow a call of their conscience in ways that are fraught with danger and disgrace. Parents who have every regard for law and order and the dictates of authority are confused when their children refuse to pay war taxes, evade the draft, take part in civil disobedience and end up in jail. Perhaps only Mary can fully understand the pain of a mother who sees her two priestly sons serving long prison sentences for destroying the instruments of mass murder. Mary can be very much one with the mother and father who wait in fear for the latest reports from a daughter or son on a Witness for Peace delegation in Nicaragua or in the missions in El Salvador. Sister Ita Ford's family and other families have faced what Mary had to face: a child's mission to challenge an entrenched power that uses its authority to control and to subjugate rather than to serve and liberate, a power that joins hands with the forces of foreign domination in order to consolidate its own power. It is a mission that ends in a degrading death.

Mary knows, too, the pain of not being able to complete a failed parenthood with at least a decent burial. She had to see her Son hurriedly laid away in a borrowed tomb with a promise to complete the rites on some future day. Mothers in the starvation camps of Somalia, mothers of the disappeared in Latin America and the Philippines, mothers whose daughters and sons are executed by the contras, may not even do so much. These mothers—and fathers— can only grieve with Mary.

Mary had to keep saying her *fiat* all her life long in all her relations with her Son. At bottom she had to accept in faith that the Father did love her Son even more than she—impossible though that seemed —and that what the Father called her Son to and what he allowed in her Son's regard was ultimately what was best for her child. Such is the heroic faith, the faith of consolation, to which Mary can lead grieving parents.

Recently a rabbi asked some of the mothers of his congregation this question: If Abraham had asked Sarah about it before he went forth obediently to sacrifice his son Isaac at God's command, what do you think Sarah would have said? Would she have encouraged Abraham in his obedience and been one with him in it? These mothers replied: No. She would have fought God for her son's life. A very understandable reaction. How often I have seen parents fight their son's monastic vocation, which they saw as a living death. Parents may well feel like fighting God for allowing the things he does allow to happen to their children. They may well be tempted to doubt his fatherly love. If Jesus cried and sweated blood in Gethsemane and struggled with his Father, don't you think Mary must have had her hours of questioning and struggle and prayed her own version of Psalm Twenty-two: My God, my God, why have you forsaken your Son and mine . . . Why does it have to be this way? Can't you do it some other way? You are God! Simeon's sword would turn and turn again. No wonder she showed her wounded heart to the seers of Fátima when she asked for reparation. But like her Son, who in the end would say, Father, not my will but yours be done, in the end there would rise up out of all the confusion, pain and anguish her perduring *fiat* and she would go on in faith and hope and love. Mary can show us the way.

Mary never failed her Son; other parents cannot be so sure. In fact, they may be quite sure that they have failed their children. (In all that I write here, and especially in this, I would include spiritual mothers and fathers.) Mary never failed her Son but she may not have been so sure of that. She may have felt that in some way she was responsible for what seemed to be going wrong in his life. She certainly felt the disgrace and pain even as, at a deeper level, she felt proud of her Son in his steadfast fidelity to his Father and his unfailing courage. Emotions were a jumble in her motherly heart at times, as they are in the hearts of all parents. She can be with us in this and teach us the confidence whereby we can firmly believe that the Father does love our daughters and sons more than we and will make up for all our lacks, known and unknown, that prevent us from doing all that needs to be done for our dear ones.

Mary is with us in all the sorrows of our hearts, a companion in pain. She can show us where to find strength and consolation.

The Woman

Literally, from end to end, from one end of the inspired Scriptures to the other, from Genesis to Revelations, we hear of *the Woman*. She is undoubtedly an important figure in God's providential plan for his creation. Indeed, in her final appearance in the Book of Revelations she takes on the stature of a cosmic figure, clothed in the sun with the moon beneath her feet.

In Genesis the Woman appears as a promise. She will bring to an end the wily serpent with all his deceitful craftiness who has inflicted such harm upon the intended stewards of creation, God's images, man and woman. But who is this Woman who will undo the harm done to woman and her mate?

In the prophetic passages the Woman could conceivably be the figure of humanity itself. Humanity, ever fruitful and bearing, brings forth seed that will have to struggle continually with the serpent, figure of all the evil spirits. Ultimately, as we find in Revelations, there will come forth from humanity, in the midst of much travail, a Child who will then have the power to rule. The end will be near at hand. But the Woman will yet have time, time to choose. Revealed as ever the consort of the Divine, she can play the harlot or she can be renewed by her Lord and become his spotless bride, his true delight.

The Chosen People, for whom the primeval promise became a covenant, saw themselves in the Woman. Chosen, yet unfaithful, one prophet after the other charged God's People with their repeated infidelity, their harlotry. Yet God's call is without repentance. He is ever faithful and true. They could return to him again and again, and each time he received them with compassion and love. Reading the prophetic story of Hosea, who was called upon to

SCA MARIA

Praying Virgin, V Century, Ravena

play out in his life the part of our faithful God, one cannot help but weep as his heart is torn again and again by an unfaithful wife.

When, at length, the promised Seed was sown in the womb of the People, the unfaithful one did not receive him. A New Covenant was struck, a new People was formed. The Woman was now the Church. Renewed in his blood, she would remain essentially faithful. Yet the temptations to infidelity are unceasing. In the course of the ensuing ages in the desert, en route to the ultimate promised land, many fall away.

The Woman, then, can be seen to be the whole of humanity as it expresses itself more specifically in a Chosen People. But in the end, most specifically, the Seed, the Child who will rule, must be borne by a particular Woman. The Gospel of John makes it clear that that woman about whom all Scripture speaks, is Mary of Nazareth. John shows her as mother and consort of the Seed, the Child, the Son of God, the eternal Word.

At Cana the Woman appears: the mother of Jesus was there— doing motherly things. In that doing, bringing a human need, there is deep symbolic meaning: a chosen but sinful people have lost all their wine of life, there is no wine left to celebrate a nuptial as the bride of God. The Woman, performing her apparently simple moth- erly act, but with a faith that did not fail to rise to another level of reality, ushered in, it sounds almost prematurely, the messianic age, the hour of the Lord, the opening of the New Covenant, the first sign of the kingdom of heaven which was now at hand, the kingdom within which the nuptials between God and his bride are to take place.

When the hour has come to its fullness and is to be completed, when wine has been changed into blood, the blood of the New Covenant, the Woman is there. Her role again is essentially that of mother: By the cross of Jesus stood his mother . . . Woman, be- hold your son. Behold the valor of this Woman! In our sexism we would be tempted to say "manly valor."

This woman is always the consort, in complete service of her Lord and his concerns, in perfect harmony with him. In the age-old battle between her Seed and the evil one, she crushes the head of the evil one. She totally humiliates this serpent, eludes his wiles and his power, preserved in a special way by her Son. It is she who brings forth the Son, amid great sufferings, so that he can go forth to rule. Her whole life, as the ancient Simeon prophesied, was one of great suffering. At Cana she will express precisely her way as consort-woman of faith: Do whatever he tells you. And thus on Calvary, in obedience to his dying wish, this Woman becomes the mother of all disciples beloved of the Lord.

Christ chose to identify himself as "the Son of Man." This is striking for, in fact, he was not the Son of any man. He was the Son of Man, a member of the human family, because he was the Son of a Woman. Through a woman he received his human nature, his family, his lineage, his city, his nation, his people, his race. It was in large measure this Woman who instilled into him his mentality, his language, his customs, his usages and his manners. It is with a woman that he has most closely identified himself in his humanity and in his mission to humanity. The desire of this Man to have a Woman intimately associated with him in the work of his life, in his generative activity, giving birth to his Church, is a sign of his integral humanity and his acceptance of the whole of humanity, female as well as male, as his own.

Jesus seems to want to emphasize the fact that Mary is "Woman." The Woman's primary role in relation to him and in relation to the community of faith, which he forms and identifies with himself as his own body, is the specifically feminine role of mother. She is mother precisely as a woman of faith, as one who courageously, openly and receptively hears the word of God and keeps it. It was by hearing the Word at the annunciation that she accepted and embraced her role as mother of Christ himself. It was by hearing his Word on Calvary that she accepted and embraced her role as mother of all the faithful.

Mother, yet virgin. In hearing the Word and embracing motherhood, Mary stood uniquely alone. There was no man who was part of her decision. She went ahead fearlessly, even as later she stood on Calvary's hill fearlessly. Depending wholly on God, she was able to be fruitful, powerful and ultimately successful without a man, yet expressing in herself those qualities we tend to ascribe to manliness. She was able to accept the less enlightened mores of her people and times but not be determined by them. She followed her own unique vocation, quietly, effectively.

Mary stands as a uniquely free and powerful woman. Her unique freedom began at the moment of her conception. Unlike any other human person who has ever been born into the family of Adam, in view of her unique mission and by the foreseen merits of her Son, she was preserved free from all domination by the evil one as well as from the passions and any evil tendency that might have bound her without this unique healing and wholing. We do not know precisely how Mary experienced this in the daily working out of her life. It did facilitate the wholeness of her yes to God. It gave her a freedom to live that yes. It gave her the freedom to be fully open to the Revelation, to receive the rich heritage of her people and to understand it deeply.

The call of God's Chosen People was a call to freedom. Abraham was called out of the bondage of idolatry and the superstitions of an unenlightened mind. God himself stooped down to be his tutor and guide and to lead him into a land and give him an inheritance where he could live freely according to the divine wisdom. Through the vicissitudes of time and the sins of the people, through a lack of appreciation of the uniqueness of their heritage and their relation with God, Abraham's family came into bondage. God sent Moses to lead them forth into freedom. He called them into covenant. They responded poorly to freedom and its responsibilities. The fleshpots of this earth and their fears ever led them back into bondage, preventing them from living in the power of their freedom. The same story was repeated again and again in the history of his people.

Mary was able to receive that freedom, its inner meaning and its true cause. She was free enough to receive it and to proclaim it in her *Magnificat*. Never has there been such a chant of freedom. It sums up all the salvific history of her people. It proclaims the way of the new covenant. It proclaims her own powerful experience of God. She is a woman who stands in the full dignity of her personhood, a worthy heir of the greatest of the prophetesses, judges, leaders, redeemers and healers of her people. The prophetess of the New Testament, proclaiming wherein true beatitude resides decades before her Son ascended the Mount of the Beatitudes.

Christianity does not aim at creating a theocracy. Christ ever evaded any move to make him a king of this world. But it does call every faithful follower of Christ forth to full freedom as a human person, commissioning us and empowering us to establish a political state wherein we can fully exercise our freedom and live according to our dignity as the freeborn children of God. This is what the apparently insignificant little Woman from "Hicksville" dared to proclaim in the heart of the hierarchy of the theocratic state, as she first bore their Liberator, all to their unknowing, into their midst. It is no wonder then that as oppressed Christians gather in base communities and source themselves again in the theology of liberation set forth in the Gospel of Jesus Christ, they look to Mary for inspiration and take up her song as their rallying chant. It is no wonder that when women stood face to face with tanks in the streets of Manila, the rosary was in their hands and the *Magnificat* on their lips.

Paul the Apostle proclaims, under the Spirit, that in Christ there is neither Jew nor Greek, slave nor free, male nor female. Everything comes together in Christ. There is no longer one Chosen People, all are called. Our creation and the primal promise, with its fulfillment in Jesus and Mary, is our title. All who have been under the bondage of sin are totally free in Christ. When we allow the grace of Christ to work fully in us, the fullness of our being the image of God reemerges, the God who is neither male nor female. We will be like Christ, the perfect image, in whom all the fullness of God dwells. He who could describe himself with motherly images and could hold another man tenderly on his heart and kiss a friend, could stand up fearlessly to any opponent, express righteous anger and not falter in the face of injustice, pain and death. Qualities which we so superficially divide between male and female are all in him as a fully integrated person and in his mother, the person most like him, the feminine expression of the same fullness. And these qualities are present in each of his disciples in so far as we are truly his disciples and allow his wholing and healing grace to do its work within us.

In Mary we find the power of the *Magnificat* and the receptivity of the *fiat*, both words of strength and courage, both bespeaking receptivity and humility.

There is neither male nor female in Mary, or rather both male and female are fully in her. There is autonomy and relatedness, strength and tenderness, struggle and victory, God's power and human agency. There is woman. She is, like her Son and by his grace and imaging, an integrated image of God. Lest by some delusion—and there is sad to say all too much delusion in our medieval catholic theology, seeping in from pagan philosophies—lest it be thought that such complete integration and imaging of Christ can only be realized in a man, God willed that there stand by Christ a perfect woman in whom this integration was fully accomplished.

As the liturgy of the New Covenant emerged, Mary stepped out from behind the synagogue screen, she stepped up from the court of the women and took her place beside the great High Priest as he entered once for all into the Holy of Holies. It is difficult, in the light of this, to understand the later exclusiveness in Christ's Church which, returning to the dispositions of the Old Covenant, seeks to exclude woman from the sanctuary. We can only conclude that age-old male dominance has consciously or unconsciously betrayed evangelical liberation. No human has ever imaged God in Christ better than a woman, the Woman.

Much has to be purged from the present predominant thinking that affects the Christian community. This thinking is a result of a truncated male outlook which has insidiously infected our theological development. Only if we get free from this bias and accept the full revelation of and call to integral humanity in Christ can Mary's full role precisely as woman be accepted, and that of all her sisters. This calls for a new humility (one of the things we have to accept is that there has never been a perfect man in creation—it took a God to be that—only a perfect woman) and vulnerability on the part of those who have held control in a faith community that has been determined by unbalanced male thinking. It calls for mutuality, reciprocity and cooperation, for autonomy in relationships, a shift from self-assertion to integration, from the rational scientific approach to the way of wisdom, open to intuition and transcendence.

The rapid emergence of women theologians offers us a most hopeful promise that this shift might begin to take place as part of the present renewal. Especially if these women can hold back from an opposite extreme which would lead them to create an unbalanced theology dominated by the feminine. We may have to live through such a reaction which, understandable though it be, would only prolong the male dominance and leave us with an official marian image which is largely a male projection. Mary has to be liberated from imaging that comes almost exclusively from male and priestly hierarchy and theologians and which hurts the true image and role of women in the Church. Feminist critique and experience do need to be heard in forming a renewed theological understanding of Mary. Just as it would be wrong to say that Jesus, because of his gender, belongs properly to men, on the assumption that we are better able by endowment to understand him, so it would be equally wrong to think that for the same reason Mary, because of her gender, belongs properly to women. There are aspects of both Jesus and Mary that women and men theologians, because of their respective genders, are better prepared to understand, enter into and bring forth into fuller light for all of us. There needs to be dialogue. Mary is a symbol of the whole human healed and reintegrated, saying a complete yes to God. When feminist theologians meet with the representatives of the male thinking, together they will produce the fully integrated image which will be the hope and inspiration of us all. Then we will see a truly New Eve at the side of the New Adam in the recapitualization of our race.

This responds to a widespread yearning in our male-dominated society, one that is hardly recognized or named, but which is, in fact, a search for the *anima*, the feminine dimension of life and being. Its unrecognized strivings are surfacing in more and more effeminate men and in increasing homosexual identification. Fear of this feminine dimension and revulsion toward it at the conscious male level makes male leadership even more suspicious and fearful of the feminine in itself and in women. An acknowledgment of the importance of the feminine and help from women to integrate it will empower men to develop an integral manhood. It is the *anima* that opens us out to the transcendent dimension of our existence. If we lack this dimension of our humanity we condemn ourselves to a rational existence, greatly limiting the role of faith in our lives. We will continue to produce a theology that is largely rational and sterile, hardly open to the transcendent, with no place for the full revelation of the Woman. Pondering will be consistently reduced to thinking and we will be deprived of the contemplative dimension of life.

Our Response

Each evening as the day draws to a close, the monks gather in abbey church for the office of Compline. They usually do not need any light as they chant the traditional psalms (4, 91, 133). They listen to the lesson and join in the prayer. Then, suddenly, as if by some heavenly magic, the great window over the high altar comes alive and the gracious mother smiles down on her children—still her children be they twenty, forty or ninety. The monks stand at attention and sing the soulful *Salve*—Hail, Holy Queen, Mother of Mercy, our life, our sweetness and our hope . . .

This is the soul of our devotion to Mary, the mother of Christ and our mother. She is our *life*, for she has brought Christ, the Way, the Truth and the Life, to us. She has birthed us in Christ and ever nurtures us.

She is *sweetness*, if we but let her into our lives. Taste and see how good the Lord is. Taste and see how good Mary is. Some things can be known only by experience. One of these is savor—sweetness. We all want it, but it can be had only by those who are willing to relax and make space for it in their lives. I know that Mary's presence has been the source of something which, if I might not spontaneously call it sweetness, makes life for me a lot "sweeter"—a lot happier, more peaceful and joyful. It is good to be loved by a woman and a mother and to be able to love her in return, to be able to talk to her freely and to share everything with her—to know that she is always available, understanding and loving. This is sweetness.

And she is our *hope*.

There is something very human here, primitive perhaps, but real. After all, our response to God is *our* response; it is, and should be,

Salve, Regina

Hail, Holy Queen,
Mother of Mercy,
our life, our sweetness and our hope,
to you do we cry,
poor banished children of Eve,
to you do we send up our sighs,
mourning and weeping
in this valley of tears.
Turn, then,
O most gracious Advocate,
your eyes of mercy toward us
and after this our exile
show unto us
the Blessed Fruit of your womb,
Jesus.
O clement,
O loving,
O sweet Virgin,
MARY!

very subjective. God did become a human so that we humans might become God's in a human way.

Scenes come back to my mind, as I am sure they do to the minds of others, from childhood. I can remember a rather stern father sending me to bed without supper. After a while, Mother would be there to see if I was tucked in all right—more to see that her little boy was all right, not too hurt or alienated. There was a word of love, and a big cookie in her apron pocket.

For many, the situation is more substantive than that. With the mounting divorce rate it is truer and truer in our own country. But it has long been the reality in Latin American countries and elsewhere. We are a fatherless people. The father is absent. Male love cannot be trusted, this is the message children receive. Hope lies with Mother.

*   *   *

THE ROSARY

I think of the rosary when I think of hope and of Mary. How many have carried the beads in their pockets or purses or have kept them in their rooms even when they have not prayed with them for years and years. The beads are there, as it were a lifeline, a chain that links with heaven. How often have I seen the beads in the hands of the sick and the dying, when strength has ebbed and words and coherent thoughts are beyond what is possible; one can still hang on to the rosary and, as it were, let it pray. I think of a great contemplative I know. He enjoys a deep, quiet, transcendent prayer, but on the occasions when I found him in the greatest anguish, I found the rosary in his hands. When a Christian lies peacefully in the coffin, usually the rosary is there in her or his hands, a mute but eloquent profession of Christian faith and hope. We believe in all the rosary mysteries and hope in their power being effective in our lives and deaths through the prayer of the mother of God: Holy Mary, Mother of God, pray for us sinners, now and at the hour of our death.

Mary was like the good householder her Son described, bringing forth from her treasures things old and new. When she chanted her great song of liberation she borrowed a lot from Anna, the mother of Samuel, bringing it forth from the great storehouse of the Scriptures. And under the Spirit she added what is new.

Legend has it that Mary herself gave St. Dominic the rosary as we know it. History seems to belie that legend. The rosary, though wholly inspired by the Gospels—we pray the prayer the Lord taught us and meditate on the basic truths of our faith—is made up of old and new.

Beads belong to women and men of every culture. They have been used to signify commitment, count prayers and focus attention in all the faiths. Some years ago I had the privilege of visiting with Kalu Rimpoche, a very wise old lama who had escaped from Tibet. All during the course of our meeting the beads moved ceaselessly through his fingers as, at a deeper level, he continued his mantra. I marveled at the chaplet that he had. It was devised to count one hundred thousand mantras.

The earliest beads in Christian history were pebbles which monks moved from one pile to another as they repeated the Jesus Prayer. Soon they wove cords of knots. This is the form that still prevails among Byzantine Christians. In the West strings of beads were devised as the layperson's psalter. As the monks, nuns and clerics chanted their hundred and fifty psalms, laypersons recited their hundred and fifty Paternosters (Our Fathers). In time, the Scripture texts that provided antiphons for the psalms chanted by the nuns and monks provided themes for meditation during the Paters. The use of the angelic salutation began to replace the Paters or be mixed with them around the time of St. Dominic (thirteenth century). The second half of the Hail Mary became common only at the time of the Reformation. It was in these centuries that decades were formed and mysteries assigned.

The beads and the words that go with them are devised to occupy our more exterior senses and thoughts, leaving our deeper places free to be with the reality beyond. We can, at times, focus all our prayer in the very touching of the beads. This can be a very simple and pure prayer, one deeply in union with Mary. In the end it is perhaps the only way we can pray the rosary.

We can concentrate on the words. The quiet repetition taking us deeper and deeper into the realities they express: Jesus . . . Mary . . . these names invoke in us the deepest emotions, words of love, names of loved ones; mother: what could be added to that word! sinners: that's us, all that that implies; the hour of our death: ultimate, final, linked with the now.

Today, the more common way to pray the rosary is to employ it to meditate discursively on fifteen basic mysteries of our Christian faith:

The Five Joyful Mysteries

1. The Annunciation
   The angel Gabriel as God's messenger asks Mary to become the mother of God and she accepts.
2. The Visitation
   Mary goes to assist her cousin, who is bearing John the Baptist.
3. The Nativity
   Jesus is born in a stable in Bethlehem.
4. The Presentation
   Jesus is presented in the temple forty days after his birth and Simeon foretells his Passion.
5. The Finding of Jesus in the Temple
   Mary and Joseph find Jesus after three days' searching.

The Five Sorrowful Mysteries

6. The Agony in the Garden
   Jesus sweats blood as he takes on our sin.
7. The Scourging at the Pillar
   Jesus is brutally scourged by the Roman soldiers.
8. The Crowning with Thorns
   Jesus is mocked as King of the Jews.
9. The Carrying of the Cross
   Jesus carries his cross to Calvary.
10. The Crucifixion
    Jesus dies on the cross.

The Five Glorious Mysteries

11. The Resurrection
    Jesus rises from the dead on the third day.
12. The Ascension
    Jesus ascends into heaven on the fortieth day after his resurrection.
13. The Descent of the Holy Spirit
    The Holy Spirit comes upon Mary and the Disciples ten days after Jesus ascended into heaven.

14. The Assumption
    The Blessed Virgin Mary is taken body and soul into heaven.
15. The Coronation
    The Blessed Virgin is crowned Queen of Heaven and Earth.

This is the way the Lady of the Rosary taught little Jacinta in the parish church in Fátima. Mary also added a prayer to be included at the end of each decade:

> O my Jesus, forgive us our sins,
> save us from the fires of hell,
> lead all souls to heaven,
> especially those who have most need of your mercy.

There are different ways in which we can approach the meditation on the mysteries. As our fingers move along the beads and our lips or minds repeat the words, we can imaginatively recall the Gospel scene and be a part of it, as an observer or as a participant, playing one role or another. We can enter into the sentiments and feelings of Jesus or Mary or others around them. We can concentrate more on the virtues Jesus and Mary are displaying in living through each particular mystery. Or we can go beyond the details and the virtues, to attend to the great basic themes that they represent: incarnation, redemption, glorification. If we will though, we can just rest in the presence of the mysteries, no thought, just loving presence.

As good householders, following Mary's example, we can bring forth new as well as the old. We can devise our own series of mysteries. The bishops of the United States in their pastoral *Behold Your Mother* encouraged us in this:

> Besides the precise rosary pattern well-known to catholics, we can freely experiment . . . new sets of mysteries are possible. We have customarily gone from the childhood of Jesus to his passion, bypassing the whole public life. There is rich material here for rosary meditation.

Thus we can meditate on other encounters of mother and Son: Cana (John 2:1–12), Jesus' visit to Nazareth (Luke 4:16–30), "Behold my mother and my brothers . . ." (Matthew 12:46–50), "Blessed is the womb . . ." (Luke 11:27–28) and at the cross (John 19:25–27).

HOW TO PRAY THE ROSARY

1. Make the Sign of the Cross and say the Apostles Creed.
2. Say the Our Father.
3. Say three Hail Marys.
4. Say the Glory be to the Father.
5. Announce the First Mystery; then say the Our Father.
6. Say ten Hail Marys, while meditating on the Mystery.
7. Say the Glory be to the Father.
8. After each decade say the following prayer requested by the Blessed Virgin Mary at Fátima: "O my Jesus, forgive us our sins, save us from the fires of hell, lead all souls to heaven, especially those who have most need of your mercy."
9. Announce the Second Mystery: then say the Our Father. Repeat 6, 7 and 8 and continue with the Third, Fourth and Fifth Mysteries in the same manner.
10. Say the Hail, Holy Queen after the five decades are completed.

As a general rule, the Joyful Mysteries are said on Monday and Thursday; the Sorrowful Mysteries on Tuesday and Friday; the Glorious Mysteries on Wednesday and Saturday. Depending on the season, each of the Mysteries is recommended for Sunday.

We can come to the tables where Jesus is teaching: Levi's (Luke 5:27–32), Simon's (Luke 7:36–50), at Bethany (Luke 10:38–42), again at Bethany (John 12:1–8) and at the Cenacle (John 13–17).

There can be healing mysteries: the first night at Simon Peter's (Mark 1:29–34), the man lowered through the roof by his friends (Mark 2:1–12), the man with the withered hand (Mark 3:1–6), the ten lepers (Luke 17:11–19) and the blind man at Jericho (Mark 10:46–52).

Or Jesus' ministry to women: the woman who touched his garment (Matthew 9:20–22), Jairus' daughter (Mark 5:21–43), the widow of Nain (Luke 7:11–17), the adulterous woman (John 8:3–11) and the sinful woman (Luke 7:36–50).

We can use the names of the Lord that are found in the Book of

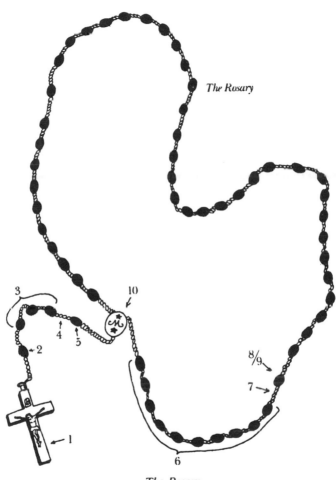

The Rosary

The Rosary

Revelations: Alpha and Omega (1:8), Lion of Judah (5:5), Son of Man (14:14), King of Kings (17:14) and Morning Star (22:16).

Or the "I am" themes in St. John's Gospel: the Bread of Life (6:35), the Gate (10:9), the Good Shepherd (10:14), the Way, the Truth and the Life (14:6) and the True Vine (15:1).

We can have resurrection mysteries: on the road to Emmaus (Luke 24:13–35), Easter night (Luke 24:36–43), a week later (John 20:24–29), by the sea (John 21:1–23) and on Olivet (Luke 24:50–53).

More subjectively we can minister to our own needs:

Preparing for reconciliation we can meditate with the rosary on "Though your sins be like scarlet, they may become white as snow" (Isaiah 1:18), "A heart contrite and humbled, O God, you will not spurn" (Psalm 51:19), "Her many sins are forgiven because of her great love" (Luke 7:47), "Neither do I condemn you" (John 8:11) and "Father, forgive them, they do not know what they are doing" (Luke 23:34).

Before approaching the Eucharist we may turn to the Eucharistic mysteries: the manna in the wilderness (Exodus 16:12), Cana (John 2:1–12), the multiplication of the loaves (John 6:1–15), the Last Supper (Mark 14:22–25) and the meal at Emmaus (Luke 24:28–32).

In a time of mourning we can find consolation in all the mysteries of our Savior and his mother, but we may choose those of his compassion: the widow of Nain (Luke 7:11–17), his tears at the tomb of Lazarus (John 11:32–44), his grief at the death of John the Baptizer (Matthew 14:3–13), his consoling the women on the way to Calvary (Luke 23:26–32) and his care for his mother (John 19:25–27).

There are many other possibilities along the lines of discursive meditation. The Scriptural Rosary, a revival of a method which was popular in the fifteenth century, has become popular again in our times. With this method a sentence from the Holy Scriptures prefixes each Hail Mary, guiding our reflection during the following prayer, just as in the Angelus.

Some years ago I had dinner in the home of a large, wealthy family. As we finished our meal, the youngest, Chris, moved around the table with a large cigar box that contained each one's dinner rosary, plus a few for guests. However, we did not pray through five mysteries (sometimes the family does that). It was the night of the Fourth Joyful Mystery. And the fourth oldest started off with her thoughts on the presentation of Jesus in the temple. The other eight children, plus Mother and Dad and the guests, joined in. At the end of a most interesting and lively sharing we prayed the decade and the Hail, Holy Queen.

The praying of the rosary usually ends with this familiar hymn to Mary. Meditating on the mysteries we know all the better that she is "our life, our sweetness and our hope." We turn to her with greater confidence, asking her help in this land of journeying and exile. From the depths of our being we sigh: O clement, O loving, O sweet Virgin, Mary.

At times we may prefer to leave thoughts aside and, letting the repetitious words serve in a sort of mantric way, rest in the center with the Lord and/or with Mary. It is enough.

It is said that Mary, in giving the rosary to St. Dominic, made many promises in regard to special care for those who used the chaplet. Be that as it may, we do know that in recent, more histori-cally established apparitions the rosary has been very present. Mary often carries the beads and prays them with the seers. At Fátima and Medjugorje, she has earnestly exhorted us to pray the rosary daily. For her, this is to be our way to peace—something we neglect to our own peril.

We are perhaps confronted with a generation without beads. The rosary used to be learned in the home at a very early age. A special rosary was given to us at the time of first communion. However, in the postconciliar turmoil the rosary has often been laid aside, hung up or lost. But the tradition is not lost. As a deacon wrote to me recently: "I have grandparents teaching their grandchildren how to pray the rosary . . . Grandparent Power." More like a venerable grandfather than a father, Patrick Peyton still proclaims widely: A family that prays together stays together. He was providentially in the Philippines, to inspire and support, when women armed only with the rosary faced tanks and won.

There is power in the rosary. But the most important power it has is its power to lead us into a deeper union with Jesus and Mary, engraving more deeply in our being the saving mysteries of our faith, the source of our hope and the cause of our love. This above all is why Mary wants us so much to pray this prayer. In our love for her, how can we fail to respond?

I do not think anyone can be faithful to the rosary and not be-come a saint. I saw it so beautifully in the life of my grandmother and my mother—whose rosary stretched out to fill the hours of her retiring years—giving them great meaning and contentment. I have seen it in the lives of many others. May the rosary be for each one of us a source of hope when Mary prays for us at the hour of our death.

THE SCAPULAR

There is a legend surrounding the black scapular the Cistercian nuns and monks wear which I rather enjoy. The founders of the monastery of Citeaux, from which the Cistercian order developed, had come from the Benedictine abbey of Molesme. Like other Benedictines of the time, they wore a black robe and a cowl—a very ample garment with long, full sleeves and hood that envelopes the monastic and disposes to interior prayer. When the monks went out to work they took off this cowl and put on a scapular, a long length of heavy wool with a hole and hood in the middle, really a sort of sweater for work time.

As the story goes, in the year 1105, on the feast of Our Lady of Snows—of which I have already spoken—Mary appeared to the monks at the night office. As a sign of her special protection—for they had dedicated their abbey to her—on this Feast of Snows she decided to change their robes and cowls from black to white. The scapulars, hanging in the work room, were not affected by this miraculous transformation. To the practical monks it seemed best to leave the scapular black to better serve their work needs. In fact, when the scapulars later became a religious symbol and almost all the religious orders adopted the practice of wearing it as part of their regular habit, the Cistercians still wore their black scapulars bound beneath their leather belts—so much more practical than having them flapping about. Practical men these monks!

It was around 1251, we are told, that Mary appeared to an English Carmelite friar, Simon Stock. She invested him in a brown scapular, assuring him that anyone who wore such a scapular would remain in a special way under her protection. It was a very typical medieval act, the vesture of a vassal, claiming service, giving protection. All monks look to Mary as their "Lady." This sign of her acceptance of them was greeted with enthusiasm. Rapidly almost all the existing orders adopted the use of the scapular and claimed Mary's promised protection.

Then as now, the friars had laypersons closely bound to them in what was called the third orders. These laypersons also wanted to receive Mary's investiture. To meet their needs, a modified form of the scapular was designed: two rectangles of wool, worn back and front, joined by narrow bands of cloth which hung over the shoulders. The Carmelite scapular was of brown wool, matching the habit of the friars. Other orders retained their respective colors. As I mentioned, the Cistercians, although they wore white robes, kept their practical black scapular. The practice developed among the Carmelite tertiaries to adorn the two rectangles of wool with pictures. The one in the front depicted Our Lady of Mount Carmel, the one in the back, Mary giving the scapular to St. Simon.

A more pragmatic age has devised an even more practical substitute for the scapular, the scapular medal, which has been approved for use by the Holy See. The medal again depicts Our Lady of Mount Carmel on one side; the other side shows Jesus exposing his Heart as a proclamation of his love. One is expected to be invested in the cloth scapular prior to using the medal.

The scapular is very meaningful to me. In 1958, on May 13, the anniversary of Mary's first apparition at Fátima, I was working on the farm, using a powerful drive shaft to operate my machine. Suddenly the shaft snatched the hem of my robe and dragged me in. Before the powerful machine had completed its work all my clothes were ripped off, including a heavy leather belt and high rubber boots, and also much of my skin. The only thing that covered my nakedness was the remnant of my scapular. I knew to whose care I owed my life and in fact, my complete salvation. Apart from the lost skin (I felt like St. Bartholomew, who was said to have been flayed alive) I was unhurt; all my bones should have been broken.

As I have said, today we can replace the scapular with a medal. And at times I do: summer's heat, swimming, exercising and so forth. But I think there is value in wearing an actual scapular, of whatever size. A medal can become too habitual. It is easy for us to lose consciousness of it. A scapular constantly needs our attention. It has to be adjusted or it gets very much awry; it has to be taken off for bathing, we can feel its wool on our backs as it moves about. Each time we become aware of it, it invites us to be aware of Mary's loving care and of our commitment to her. Sacramentals are for our sake, so we should use them in the way that will best help us. To experience ourselves constantly under Mary's care can be a very consoling and strengthening gift on the journey.

THE MIRACULOUS MEDAL

While a scapular arrests our attention more, medals can and do serve. Just as in the Middle Ages it was natural for a vassal to be invested by his lord or lady, so too is it quite natural for us to wear pendants, pendants of affiliation, pendants of love. The medals that we wear depicting Mary may be our lockets, declaring our love, proclaiming that we belong to her. Although there are many different medals we can wear to declare these realities, there is one special one that also declares Mary's love and care for us. This is the so-called miraculous medal which Mary herself designed and asked Catherine Labouré to have executed and distributed among her children. The multitude of miracles associated with its use tell of the extraordinary care on the part of Mary for those who wear this medal.

We might be tempted to ask why, when so many miracles were associated with the medal's use in its early days, there are no miracles being reported today. In fact, there are still some reports of miracles among the thousands and thousands of pilgrims who visit the Rue de Bac each year, and also elsewhere. Perhaps they are few in comparison to those first days because we do not seek miracles. I know that I have never sought one in all the years that I have worn the medal. Or maybe, in God's design, the flood of early miracles was meant to advertise the medal and win its acceptance. Many of us who use the medal do not seek "special" miracles but confidently expect that everyday protection and care that Mary promised to those who wear the medal.

THE DEVOTION OF THE FIVE FIRST SATURDAYS

This is a relatively new devotion in honor of the Blessed Virgin or, more exactly, to make reparation to her Immaculate Heart.

What is reparation? I believe reparation involves two elements. First, it is an awareness and acknowledgment that I have caused another pain; then, it is an effort to try to make amends for that pain.

This devotion of the five first Saturdays originated at Fátima. There, following the example of her Son, who had exposed his Sacred Heart earlier at Paray-le-Monial, Mary showed her heart to the children and told them of the pain and sorrow she suffered because of our sins. She went on to ask for reparation and explained the form she wanted it to take.

It may strike us as strange that Mary would ask for reparation. It seems to me we might see it as a mother trying to teach us the importance of acting as we ought, in justice and truth, with an eye to what is due her Son. We have all seen a mother who has given her child something, insisting that the child say thank you. The mother, in demanding this, is not concerned for herself. She only wants her child to learn to act properly and to develop a sense of gratitude. Reparation is a basic human good. It flows from a sense of justice, if not love, and it instills these virtues in us. I think if we examine ourselves we will find that we are fairly weak in our sense of reparation. Even when we say we are sorry, we are often slow to make amends. This is probably most true in our response to Mary's Son. Yet we know that when we truly love people and we hurt them, we are most eager to do whatever we can to make it up. Mary our Mother wants us to be truly and happily just: Blessed are they who hunger and thirst after justice . . . So she, as a mother, seeks to put us through our paces. We have indeed inflicted pain on Mary in so far as we have done this to her Son by our sins. For us he hung on Calvary's hill, after living all his life for us. All the sorrow she bore at his side was for us. We have plenty for which to make reparation: our every sin, and above all our unconsciousness and ingratitude.

There is another element here, too. Mary knows that our offering reparation to her will please her Son. And she wants him to be pleased and to be pleased with us. Hence, her motherly demand.

Mary tells us precisely what to do to make the due reparation. We are to go to mass and receive holy communion, pray the rosary and meditate for fifteen minutes: public devotion and private devotion, active prayer and contemplative prayer. Even as sin distances us from her Son, the reparation she asks is to draw us close to him. Even as our sin diminishes our spiritual strength, her proposed reparation will build it up again. The reparation that Mary asks is not to her profit but to ours. This is a mother's way and brings joy to her heart.

Mary asked we do this for five consecutive first Saturdays—more modest than the nine first Fridays requested by her Son. In fact, while five are minimal, we poor sinners will find that we cannot stop there. We keep on sinning in ways little if not great and so we have to keep offering reparation. If we have learned our lesson about being just and making reparation, we will probably be observing the first Saturdays of each month for the rest of our lives. Each time, perhaps, learning a little more about justice. Each time, perhaps, healing not only the offense done to Mary and the pain we caused her, but healing our own wounds of sin.

These devotions are all particularizations of basic human qualities, influenced by our faith as enlivened by tradition and the apparitions of Mary. The most basic devotion was instilled by Mary at Tepeyac: accepting her as merciful mother and loving her gratefully in return.

THE ANGELUS

My work was just interrupted by the sound of the great bell in the abbey tower. It was noontime and the bell gave forth a rather particular ring: three strokes, three strokes, three strokes and a longish peel. It was the noonday Angelus. Three times a day the bells ring out like this. When they do, all activity comes to a halt, all turn toward the church and pray. Before the "renewal," we used to prostrate on our knees and knuckles in the same way that Scripture describes the prophet Daniel prostrating toward the Holy City of Jerusalem during his daily prayer. It is a special moment.

I grew up in a parish where the Angelus was a living practice. Sam, the sacristan, morning, noon and night, rang the familiar ring. The noncatholics called it the friendship bell. They would stop and greet each other, sometimes hugging or shaking hands. We catholics knew it was, indeed, the friendship bell: it commemorated the most important moment in all history when God became man to be the friend of women and men: I no longer call you servants but friends . . .

The Angelus is a scriptural prayer. Its verses come from the all-important dialogue Mary had with the Archangel Gabriel and from St. John's description of the result of that dialogue. We join the angel in saluting Mary and ask her to pray for us.

The Angelus

The angel of the Lord declared unto Mary,
And she conceived of the Holy Spirit.
Hail, Mary . . . .
Behold the handmaid of the Lord,

Be it done unto me according to your word.
Hail, Mary . . .
The Word was made Flesh,
And dwelt among us.
Hail, Mary . . .
Pray for us, O holy Mother of God,
That we may be made worthy of the promises of Christ.

Let us pray.

Pour forth, we beseech you, O Lord, your grace into our hearts, that we to whom the Incarnation of your divine Son was made known by the message of an angel, may by his Passion and Cross be brought to the glory of his Resurrection, who lives and reigns forever and ever. Amen.

These devotions honoring Mary are all sources of hope for us. They increase our awareness of how much we are loved and they increase our love. They are occasions of increased faith.

We can bring Mary into other devotions, such as the ancient practice of the Stations of the Cross. The mother of Jesus appears early on the journey to Calvary. She was undoubtedly present in the background since the start. We can walk the *Via Dolorosa* with the *Mater Dolorosa*. She, more than anyone, can lead us into the deepest understanding of it.

If Mary was so present at the actual enactment of our redemption on Calvary then she is present in each celebration of the mass, for the mass is Calvary drawn from the eternal now of God and made present here and now by the liturgical ritual which the Lord himself gave us to effect this. Here again, Mary is not essentially different from us, just preeminent. Each of us can bring to Calvary's sacrifice our own co-offering. And the love and presence we bring will be made one with our Head's and be forever part of his offering as it is renewed again and again through the ages. Mary is present to show us how to be co-offerers as well as recipients. No one has been so open and received as fully the redeeming grace that flows from Calvary as has the Holy Mother of God. She can, indeed, teach us how to receive that grace.

Surrounding this central act of our liturgy is the yearly cycle in which we relive the mysteries of Jesus and Mary and commemorate certain aspects of their loving presence to us. Like the rosary, the cycle of feasts invites us to enter more deeply into the basis of our faith, hope and love. The liturgy gives a certain actuality to the presence of these events. It facilitates our entering into and receiving the grace of each. Commemorating Mary's apparitions at Guadalupe (December 12), Lourdes (February 11), Paris (November 27) and Fátima, with the Feast of the Immaculate Heart of Mary, renews the graces of these visits in us. In doing this, we do it as a people supported by all the Church, sharing with all the Church. Everything is in place to build up our faith and hope and love.

True Devotion

What return can we make unto Mary for all that she has done and is doing for us? There is nothing Mary wants more than to please her Son who is her God. For her the two great commandments come together as one in that Boy of hers. We hear in Scripture of only one request Jesus made of her, made in the supreme moment of his life and mission: Woman, behold your son, your child. We can do nothing to please Mary more than to do what her Son did and wants— entrust ourselves completely to her as her children. We accept Jesus' gift of his mother and place ourselves under her care to keep close to her Son, to be conformed to him in doing what always pleases the Father, ever open to the Holy Spirit who will teach us all things, calling to mind all that Jesus has said to us.

St. Louis Grignon de Montfort popularized a form of devotion to Mary which he called "true devotion." In the beginning of this book I shared how embracing this practice set forth by St. Louis radically altered the course of my life. It is a grace for which I can never thank God enough. De Montfort, in the exaggerated style of his time and place, speaks of giving ourselves to Mary as slaves. I do not think that is precisely what Mary our mother wants. Her Son spoke of beloved disciples being accepted by her as sons. Nevertheless, the totality of the gift that St. Louis wished to underline has its place. With total confidence, we turn ourselves over to Mary's care, just as did God in his incarnation; we wish, like the young Jesus, to remain subject to her. We do not wish to outgrow this subjection, for unless we be as little ones we cannot enter the kingdom. So said her Son, our Lord. Moreover, just as Jesus has willed that the totality of the divine creative action that is grace flow from his redeeming sacrifice first into Mary and then, through her and in accord with her disposition, into the rest of us, so we turn over to our mother and his the determination of all the grace that flows through our lives. We are hers and hers we want to be—knowing that all that is hers is most precious to her Son. We live out this consecration, this giving of ourselves to Jesus through Mary with a gentle, peaceful, joyful consciousness that there is no surer way for us to please her Son and to receive the grace to do always the things that please the Father.

We do not need high-flown theology or depth psychology to comprehend this devotion, only an understanding heart.

With Mary we give all glory to Father in the Son through the Holy Spirit. This is true devotion. This we renew each morning as we begin our day praying:

O Jesus,
through the Immaculate Heart of Mary
I offer you
all my prayers, works, joys and suffering
of this day . . .

EPILOGUE

The Challenging Woman

We live in one of the most threatened times, if not *the* most threatened time, in the history of the human family. In the midst of our profound concern, which is leading many into despair with little care for the morrow, Mary offers us hope and challenge.

In face of the world situation where there are wars and rumors of war and always the threat of the inconceivable global devastation of a nuclear war, Mary, the Queen of Peace, challenges us with a peace plan which she presented first at Fátima and has reiterated at Medjugorje. It is simple and clear:

We are to build up our faith, hope and love by daily prayer—not just words but meditation on the basic mysteries of our faith as we do in praying the rosary. Then we are to offer reparation in the light of our renewed faith, realizing how much we have offended God. In love we seek to make amends, entering into Christ's great sacrifice of reparation through holy communion.

In doing this, we will find great peace and joy. Then we can be effective instruments of peace. If every Christian followed this peace plan, how could there not be peace on earth?

I believe that Mary offers a special challenge to the United States Church and to its leaders. We are challenged to lead the way in creating an integrated society within the Church in which all the children of God are accepted, respected and make their contribution. Our Church proclaims its option for the poor. In this it shares the heart of the Virgin of the Poor. This option cannot be restricted to those who are poor in dollars and cents, pesos or lire. It must also include, with great compassion, those who lead deeply deprived lives because they have been marginalized, impoverished because of prejudice and discrimination.

There can be a theological arrogance that would set up the theology that uses the Greco-Roman philosophical outlook of scholasticism in a search for understanding the Revelation as *the* theology normative for all others—normative almost in the way that only the inspired Sacred Scriptures should be our norm. We are Roman Catholics. That does not mean we have to be Roman in our philosophical outlook. Our outlook is to be catholic—universal, embracing the valid philosophies of all people as useful in our faith-filled quest for understanding. As the Indians of India, inspired by the Spirit-filled directives of the Second Vatican Council, begin to use the traditional wisdom and philosophy of their people and culture to develop theological understanding, as the Japanese do the same, and the Africans, so we in the United States cannot afford to hamper our theological quest by limiting ourselves to the use of a Greco-Roman philosophical system. There is alive among the United States catholics not only the existential philosophical outlook of the "Yankee" community—the philosophical approach that has made Thomas Merton the most powerful and effective voice in American catholicism—but the rich earthy philosophy coming out of the lived experience and inherited cultures of the large Hispanic dimension of the United States catholic community. We see this heritage giving expression, in the base communities of Latin America, to a liberation theology very consonant with the underlying biblical thrust that stretches from Exodus to Calvary. In the United States, this rich heritage with all its theological potential flows together with, or should be allowed to flow together with, older or more recent European, Asiatic, African and Native American traditions which other segments of our one United States Church bring to a common theological inquiry.

The United States Church has the potential to make an extraordinarily rich contribution to the development of doctrine and worship within the universal catholic Church and the world Christian community because of this confluence, if it is faithful to its best national heritage by being the place where the riches of all peoples can come together to form one people. The deeper message that Mary conveyed when she sent Juan Diego to the Spanish bishop of Mexico City, portraying herself as an Aztec maiden, must be heard by the bishops of the United States today as they guide the theological inquiry and liturgical development within our national Church and bring that contribution to the universal Church. Otherwise they will not only truncate our growth and fail to make a much needed contribution, they will also lose the millions whose ancestors flocked to Christ and to the Church when the Maiden of Guadalupe opened the door.

Only when we, as a Christian community, show such respect for our own marginalized and needy members can we hope to bring a ministry to the poor that will be worthy of them as God's chosen—as the Christ in our midst today.

In the ongoing development of the doctrine concerning the Blessed Virgin Mary and of her meaning as the Woman, a woman in our Church, we are building one of the greatest of all marian cathedrals. Like the episcopal cathedral of St. John the Divine in New York, the work is still incomplete. That great cathedral in Manhattan has lots of people space and it is open to all sorts of events, some a bit shocking to our more refined ecclesiastical sensibilities. Yet it is the cathedral that is succeeding to gather in the people of God in ways that no other cathedral does. Someday it will perhaps stand complete, the largest and most glorious of the world's Gothic cathedrals, exalted on the heights (significantly it is built on the crest of Morningside Heights), yet still rooted solidly in the teeming masses of the world's richest metropolis, rich in people and cultures and life as well as in wealth, influence and connections.

When the full mystery of Mary is set forth her exaltation will not be alienating as it is now sometimes experienced. The felt need now of many, as I have already mentioned, is that she be more in our midst. Such a wonderfully human woman, who is rightly identified with the marginalized, may leave some of the more ecclesiastically minded, who are more comfortable with her enthroned over the portal in the tympanum or in the Lady chapel, feeling rather uncomfortable.

In many different ways Mary challenges each one of us to be better disciples. To hear the Word of God and keep it in all that we say and do. To expand and sensitize our response to our brothers and sisters. To be attentive to needs great and small, to have a compassionate and caring heart, a courageous heart that stands with the needy and oppressed. At Cana we see her bustling about, concerned that there be enough wine to truly celebrate new life. Earlier at Elizabeth's, in the midst of the privileged, she gives powerful expression, one deeply rooted in God and his revelation, to a heartfelt concern for the poor, for the oppressed, for the hungry of the world. Mary is a liberator: she brought our Liberator to us, she proclaims him the Liberator, and she stands with him solidly on the side of the oppressed.

Mary challenges us to open to the full meaning and role of women in our Church and in our world. And she challenges women to take their role and fulfill it with courage for the well-being of us all. As a woman, Mary had the courage to be a mother. It takes a lot of courage to bring a child into this world today and to be ever present to that child no matter what happens. Mary had the courage to be a virgin. How many young women today would dare to proclaim themselves a virgin, standing in their native dignity, not allowing themselves to be used? Mary dared to proclaim her true dignity, her God-given role among the people of God, even among those who could or would not understand and would probably respond with derision. Mary dared to stand by the side of her Son when he allowed himself to be totally identified with the oppressed, disgraced and degraded. Mary stayed, a source of strength and peace, in the midst of the disciples, as a woman teaching them more by example than by word how to open themselves through prayer and waiting for the coming empowerment of the Spirit. Before a man can make the journey into the full power of his masculinity— and not just stay with the defensive macho shell of a pseudo masculinity—he has to have the courage and help of a woman to make the journey into his own femininity.

Mary is the woman, the archetype of the persons we are to be as Christians. She challenges us to open ourselves to experience our humanity in its fullness, to let both our masculinity and our femininity emerge, to be whole persons who create a whole Church, allowing the fullness of humanity to be divinized within it.

Mary challenges us to face the ordinariness of our lives and to believe in the ordinariness of our lives. It was in leading, for the most part, a very ordinary life that she fulfilled the greatest mission that has ever been given to a human person and that she prepared herself for those times when she would, in some way, have to step out of the ordinary and perform the heroic.

Mary challenges us to walk in her way, the way of the yes of love. Her advice to us: Do whatever he tells you.

Mary has urged us to pray the rosary daily, to spend time in meditation, to fast, to take part in the Eucharist, to offer Saturdays of reparation, to wear the scapular and the miraculous medal. She is a mother; she knows our needs. She is seeking to respond to each one of them. She wants us to discern under the Spirit what will help us as individuals, to use the means that will, to be faithful in our use of them and to grow.

In the final pages of the written revelation, Mary appears great and glorious. She is clothed with the sun, the moon is under her feet and on her head is a crown of twelve stars. She is the bride who comes before the Lamb, all beautiful and spotless. And yet she disappears. She willingly fades into the background. That heavenly city has no need of sun and moon, for the glory of God gives it its light and its lamp is the Lamb. The throne of God and the Lamb is there and all his servants serve him faithfully. And Mary, happily in their midst, says again: Behold the handmaid of the Lord. If I have been most privileged and have a glory beyond compare among his servants, it is because he who is mighty has done great things for me. Holy is his Name.

Mary challenges us to a selflessness that seeks nothing but that our lives and our being should magnify the Lord.

Who is Mary?

At the risk of it sounding like a cliché or a cop-out, I would say the best answer to that question is silence (after writing a whole book!). If biblical exegetes could leave aside for a moment historical criticism and quiet their rational mind they might find how ultimately empty is all that they have been saying. If pained feminists could sit for a bit in silence with this Woman, their anger would soften and be healed. If any one of us would enter into the silence of Mary's presence we would find healing for our woundedness, solace in our loneliness, our emptiness would be filled up and our lives would magnify the Lord. At the beginning of this writing I wanted to sing of a maiden, now I would enter into the silence of a Woman who ponders all things in her heart.

Ever Virgin Mary
    MOTHER
        of all peoples
        nations far and near
            universal
and onetwothreefourfive little children of her own
                                each
She is of exalted beauty
          and what I want to know is
how the WOMAN so great and glorious
can love me.
                       She does.

APPENDIX

The Light of the Nations

CHAPTER VIII
OUR LADY

I. Introduction

52. Wishing in his supreme goodness and wisdom to effect the redemption of the world, "when the fullness of time came, God sent his Son, born of a woman . . . that we might receive the adoption of sons" (Gal. 4:4). "He for us, and for our salvation, came down from heaven, and was incarnated by the Holy Spirit from the Virgin Mary."[1] This divine mystery of salvation is revealed to us and continued in the Church, which the Lord established as his body. Joined to Christ the head and in communion with all his saints, the faithful must in the first place reverence the memory "of the glorious ever Virgin Mary, Mother of God and of our Lord Jesus Christ."[2]

53. The Virgin Mary, who at the message of the angel received the Word of God in her heart and in her body and gave Life to the world, is acknowledged and honored as being truly the Mother of God and of the redeemer. Redeemed, in a more exalted fashion, by reason of the merits of her Son and united to him by a close and indissoluble tie, she is endowed with the high office and dignity of the Mother of the Son of God, and therefore she is also the beloved daughter of the Father and the temple of the Holy Spirit. Because of this gift of sublime grace she far surpasses all creatures, both in heaven and on earth. But, being of the race of Adam, she is at the same time also united to all those who are to be saved; indeed, "she

1. Creed of the Roman mass; Symbol of Constantinople: Mansi 3, 566. Cf. Council of Ephesus; ibid. 4, 1130 *(et ibid.* 2, 665 and 4, 1071); Council of Chalcedon, ibid. 7, 111–116; Council of Constantinople II. ibid. 9, 375–396.
2. Canon of the Roman Mass.

is clearly the mother of the members of Christ . . . since she has by her charity joined in bringing about the birth of believers in the Church, who are members of its head."[3] Wherefore she is hailed as pre-eminent and as a wholly unique member of the Church, and as its type and outstanding model in faith and charity. The Catholic Church taught by the Holy Spirit, honors her with filial affection and devotion as a most beloved mother.

54. Wherefore this sacred synod, while expounding the doctrine on the Church, in which the divine Redeemer brings about our salvation, intends to set forth painstakingly both the role of the Blessed Virgin in the mystery of the Incarnate Word and the Mystical Body, and the duties of the redeemed towards the Mother of God, who is mother of Christ and mother of men, and most of all those who believe. It does not, however, intend to give a complete doctrine on Mary, nor does it wish to decide those questions which the work of theologians has not yet fully clarified. Those opinions therefore may be lawfully retained which are propounded in Catholic schools concerning her, who occupies a place in the Church which is the highest after Christ and also closest to us.[4]

II. *The Function of the Blessed Virgin*
in the Plan of Salvation

55. The sacred writings of the Old and New Testaments, as well as venerable tradition, show the role of the Mother of the Saviour in the plan of salvation in an ever clearer light and call our attention to it. The books of the Old Testament describe the history of salvation, by which the coming of Christ into the world was slowly prepared. The earliest documents, as they are read in the Church and are understood in the light of a further and full revelation, bring the figure of a woman, Mother of the Redeemer, into a gradually clearer light. Considered in this light, she is already prophetically foreshadowed in the promise of victory over the serpent which was given to our first parents after their fall into sin (cf. Gen. 3:15). Likewise she is the virgin who shall conceive and bear a son, whose name shall be called Emmanuel (cf. Is. 8:14; Mic. 5:2–3; Mt. 1:22–23). She stands out among the poor and humble of the Lord, who confidently hope for and receive salvation from him. After a long period of waiting

3. Cf. St. Augustine, *De S. Virginitate*, 6: *PL* 40, 399.
4. Cf. Paul VI, *Allocution to the Council*, 4 December 1963: *AAS* 56 (1964), p. 37.

the times are fulfilled in her, the exalted Daughter of Sion and the new plan of salvation is established, when the Son of God has taken human nature from her, that he might in the mysteries of his flesh free us from sin.

56. The Father of mercies willed that the Incarnation should be preceded by assent on the part of the predestined mother, so that just as a woman had a share in bringing about death, so also a woman should contribute to life. This is preeminently true of the Mother of Jesus, who gave to the world the Life that renews all things, and who was enriched by God with gifts appropriate to such a role. It is no wonder then that it was customary for the Fathers to refer to the Mother of God as all holy and free from every stain of sin, as though fashioned by the Holy Spirit and formed as a new creature.[5] Enriched from the first instant of her conception with the splendor of an entirely unique holiness, the virgin of Nazareth is hailed by the heralding angel, by divine command, as "full of grace" (cf. Lk. 1:28), and to the heavenly messenger she replies: "Behold the handmaid of the Lord, be it done unto me according to thy word" (Lk. 1:38). Thus the daughter of Adam, Mary, consenting to the word of God, became the Mother of Jesus. Committing herself whole-heartedly to God's saving will and impeded by no sin, she devoted herself totally, as a handmaid of the Lord, to the person and work of her Son, under and with him, serving the mystery of redemption, by the grace of Almighty God. Rightly, therefore, the Fathers see Mary not merely as passively engaged by God, but as freely cooperating in the work of our salvation through faith and obedience. For, as St Irenaeus says, she "being obedient, became the cause of salvation for herself and for the whole human race."[6] Hence not a few of the early Fathers gladly assert with him in their preaching: "the knot of Eve's disobedience was untied by Mary's obedience: what the virgin Eve bound through her disbelief, Mary loosened by her faith."[7] Comparing Mary with Eve, they call her

5. Cf. Germanus of Constantinople, *Hom. in Annunt. Deiparae: PG* 98, 328A; *In Dorm.* 2, Col. 357. Anastasius of Antioch. *Serm.* 2 *de Annunt.* 2: *PG* 89, 1377 AB; *Serm.* 3. 2: Col. 1388 C. St. Andrew of Crete, *Can. in B.V. Nat.* 4: *PG* 97, 1321 B. *In B.V. Nat.* 1: Col. 812 A. *Hom. in Dorm.* 1: Col. 1068C. St. Sophronius, *Or.* 2 *in Annunt.* 18: *PG* 87 (3), 3237 BD.

6. St. Irenaeus, *Adv. Haer.* III, 22, 4: *PG* 7, 959 A, Harvey, 2, 123.

7. St. Irenaeus, ibid.: Harvey, 2, 124.

"Mother of the living,"[8] and frequently claim: "death through Eve, life through Mary."[9]

57. This union of the mother with the Son in the work of salvation is made manifest from the time of Christ's virginal conception up to his death; first when Mary, arising in haste to go to visit Elizabeth, is greeted by her as blessed because of her belief in the promise of salvation and the precursor leaped with joy in the womb of his mother (cf. Lk. 1:41–45); then also at the birth of Our Lord, who did not diminish his mother's virginal integrity but sanctified it,[10] the Mother of God joyfully showed her firstborn son to the shepherds and the Magi: when she presented him to the Lord in the temple, making the offering of the poor, she heard Simeon foretelling at the same time that her Son would be a sign of contradiction and that a sword would pierce the mother's soul, that out of many hearts thoughts might be revealed (cf. Lk. 2:34–35); when the child Jesus was lost and they had sought him sorrowing, his parents found him in the temple, engaged in the things that were his Father's, and they did not understand the words of their Son. His mother, however, kept all these things to be pondered in her heart (cf. Lk. 2:41–51).

58. In the public life of Jesus Mary appears prominently; at the very beginning when at the marriage feast of Cana, moved with pity, she brought about by her intercession the beginning of miracles of Jesus the Messiah (cf. Jn. 2:1–11). In the course of her Son's preaching she received the words whereby, in extolling a kingdom beyond the concerns and ties of flesh and blood, he declared blessed those who heard and kept the word of God (cf. Mk. 3:35; par. Lk. 11:27–27) as she was faithfully doing (cf. Lk. 2:19; 51). Thus the Blessed Virgin advanced in her pilgrimage of faith, and faithfully persevered in her union with her Son unto the cross, where she stood, in keeping with the divine plan, enduring with her only begotten Son the intensity of his suffering, associated herself with his sacrifice in her mother's heart, and lovingly consenting to the immolation of

---

8. St. Epiphanius, *Haer.* 78, 18: *PG* 42, 728 CD–729 AB.

9. St. Jerome, *Epist.* 22, 21: *PL* 22, 408. Cf. St. Augustine, *Serm.* 51, 2, 3: *PL* 38, 335; *Serm.* 232, 2: Col. 1108. St. Cyril, of Jerusalem, *Catech.* 12, 15: *PG* 33, 741 AB. St. John Chrysostom, *In Ps.* 44, 7: *PG* 55, 193. St. John Damascene, *Hom. 2 in dorm. B.M.V.*, 3: *PG* 96, 728.

10. Cf. Council of Lateran A.D. 649, Can. 3: Mansi 10, 1151. St. Leo the Great, *Epist. ad Flav.: PL* 54, 759. Council of Chalcedon: Mansi 7, 462. St. Ambrose, *De instit. virg.: PL* 16, 320.

this victim which was born of her. Finally, she was given by the same Christ Jesus dying on the cross as a mother to his disciple, with these words: "Woman, behold thy son" (Jn. 19:26–27).[11]

59. But since it had pleased God not to manifest solemnly the mystery of the salvation of the human race before he would pour forth the Spirit promised by Christ, we see the apostles before the day of Pentecost "persevering with one mind in prayer with the women and Mary the Mother of Jesus, and with his brethren" (Acts 1:14), and we also see Mary by her prayers imploring the gift of the Spirit, who had already overshadowed her in the Annunciation. Finally the Immaculate Virgin preserved free from all stain of original sin,[12] was taken up body and soul into heavenly glory,[13] when her earthly life was over, and exalted by the Lord as Queen over all things, that she might be the more fully conformed to her Son, the Lord of lords, (cf. Apoc. 19:16) and conqueror of sin and death.[14]

III. *The Blessed Virgin and the Church*

60. In the words of the apostle there is but one mediator: "for there is but one God and one mediator of God and men, the man Christ Jesus, who gave himself a redemption for all" (1 Tim. 2:5–6). But Mary's function as mother of men in no way obscures or diminishes this unique mediation of Christ, but rather shows its power. But the Blessed Virgin's salutary influence on men originates not in any inner necessity but in the disposition of God. It flows forth from the superabundance of the merits of Christ, rests on his mediation, depends entirely on it and draws all its power from it. It does not hinder in any way the immediate union of the faithful with Christ but on the contrary fosters it.

61. The predestination of the Blessed Virgin as Mother of God was associated with the incarnation of the divine word: in the de-

11. Cf. Pius XII, Encycl. *Mystici Corporis*, 29 June 1943: *AAS* 35 (1943), pp. 247–248.

12. Cf. Pius IX, Bull *Ineffabilis*, 8 Dec. 1854: *Acta Pii IX*, 1, 1, p. 616; *Denz.* 1641 (2803).

13. Cf. Pius XII, Const. Apost. *Munificentissimus*, 1 Nov. 1950: *AAS* 42 (1950): *Denz.* 2333 (3903). Cf. St. John Damascene, *Enc. in dorm. Dei Genitricis, Hom.* 2 and 3: *PG* 96, 722–762, esp. Col. 728 B. St. Germanus of Constantinople, *In S. Dei gen. dorm. Serm.* 1: *PG* 78 (6), 340–348; *Serm.* 3: Col. 362. St. Modestus of Jerusalem, *In dorm. SS. Deiparae: PG* 86 (2), 3277–3312.

14. Cf. Pius XII, Encycl. *Ad coeli Reginam*, 11 Oct. 1954: *AAS* 46 (1954), pp. 633–636: *Denz.* 3914 ff. Cf. St. Andrew of Crete, *Hom. 3 in dorm. SS Deiparae: PG* 97, 1090–1109. St. John Damascene, *De fide orth.*, IV, 14: *PG* 94, 1153–1168.

signs of divine Providence she was the gracious mother of the divine Redeemer here on earth, and above all others and in a singular way the generous associate and humble handmaid of the Lord. She conceived, brought forth, and nourished Christ, she presented him to the Father in the temple, shared her Son's sufferings as he died on the cross. Thus, in a wholly singular way she cooperated by her obedience, faith, hope and burning charity in the work of the Savior in restoring supernatural life to souls. For this reason she is a mother to us in the order of grace.

62. This motherhood of Mary in the order of grace continues uninterruptedly from the consent which she loyally gave at the Annunciation and which she sustained without wavering beneath the cross, until the eternal fulfilment of all the elect. Taken up to heaven she did not lay aside this saving office but by her manifold intercession continues to bring us the gifts of eternal salvation.[15] By her maternal charity, she cares for the brethren of her Son, who still journey on earth surrounded by dangers and difficulties, until they are led into their blessed home. Therefore the Blessed Virgin is invoked in the Church under the titles of Advocate, Helper, Benefactress, and Mediatrix.[16] This, however, is so understood that it neither takes away anything from nor adds anything to the dignity and efficacy of Christ the one Mediator.[17]

No creature could ever be counted along with the Incarnate Word and Redeemer; but just as the priesthood of Christ is shared in various ways both by his ministers and the faithful, and as the one goodness of God is radiated in different ways among his creatures, so also the unique mediation of the Redeemer does not exclude but rather gives rise to a manifold cooperation which is but a sharing in this one source.

The Church does not hesitate to profess this subordinate role of Mary, which it constantly experiences and recommends to the heartfelt attention of the faithful, so that encouraged by this maternal

15. Cf. Kleutgen, corrected text *De mysterio verbi incarnati*, ch. IV: Mansi 53, 290. Cf. St. Andrew of Crete, *In nat. Mariae, Serm.* 4: *PG* 97, 865 A. St. Germanus of Constantinople, *In ann. Deiparae: PG* 93, 322 BC. *In dorm. Deiparae* III: Col. 362 D. St. John Damascene, *In dorm B.V.M., Hom.* 1, 8: *PG* 96, 712 BC-713 A.

16. Cf. Leo XIII, Encycl. *Adjutricem populi,* 5 Sept. 1895: *AAS* 15 (1895–1896), p. 303. St. Pius X, Encycl. *Ad diem illum,* 2 Feb. 1904: *Acta* 1, p. 154; *Denz.* 1978a (3370). Pius XI, Encycl. *Miserentissimus,* 8 May 1928; *AAS* 20 (1928), p. 178. Pius XII, Radio Message, 13 May 1946: *AAS* 38 (1946), p. 268.

17. St. Ambrose, *Epist.* 63: *PL* 16, 1218.

help they may the more closely adhere to the Mediator and Redeemer.

63. By reason of the gift and role of her divine motherhood, by which she is united with her Son, the Redeemer, and with her unique graces and functions, the Blessed Virgin is also intimately united to the Church. As St. Ambrose taught, the Mother of God is a type of the Church in the order of faith, charity, and perfect union with Christ.[18] For in the mystery of the Church, which is itself rightly called mother and virgin, the Blessed Virgin stands out in eminent and singular fashion as exemplar both of virgin and mother.[19] Through her faith and obedience she gave birth on earth to the very Son of the Father, not through the knowledge of man but by the overshadowing of the Holy Spirit, in the manner of a new Eve who placed her faith, not in the serpent of old but in God's messenger without wavering in doubt. The Son whom she brought forth is he whom God placed as the first born among many brethren (Rom. 8:29), that is, the faithful, in whose generation and formation she cooperates with a mother's love.

64. The Church indeed contemplating her hidden sanctity, imitating her charity and faithfully fulfilling the Father's will, by receiving the word of God in faith becomes herself a mother. By preaching and baptism she brings forth sons, who are conceived of the Holy Spirit and born of God, to a new and immortal life. She herself is a virgin, who keeps in its entirety and purity the faith she pledged to her spouse. Imitating the mother of her Lord, and by the power of the Holy Spirit, she keeps intact faith, firm hope and sincere charity.[20]

65. But while in the most Blessed Virgin the Church has already reached that perfection whereby she exists without spot or wrinkle (cf. Eph. 5:27), the faithful still strive to conquer sin and increase in holiness. And so they turn their eyes to Mary who shines forth to the whole community of the elect as the model of virtues. Devoutly meditating on her and contemplating her in the light of the Word

---

18. Ambrose, *Expos. Lc. II.* 7: *PL* 15, 1555.
19. Cf. Pseudo Peter Damien, *Serm.* 63: *PL* 144, 861 AB. Geoffrey (de Breteuil) of St. Victor, *In nat. b.m.*, MS. Paris, Mazarine, 1002, fol. 109. Gerhoch of Reichersberg, *De gloria et honore Filii hominis* 10: *PL* 194, 1105AB.
20. St. Ambrose, l.c., and *Expos. Lc. X*, 24–25: *PL* 15, 1810. St. Augustine, *In Io. Tr.* 13. 12: *PL* 35, 1499. Cf. *Serm.* 191, 2, 3: *PL* 38, 1010, etc. Cf. also Ven. Bede, *In Lc. Expo.*, 1, ch. II: 92, 330. Isaac of Stella, *Serm.* 31: *PL* 194, 1863 A. 21. "*Sub tuum praesidium.*"

made man, the Church reverently penetrates more deeply into the great mystery of the Incarnation and becomes more and more like her spouse. Having entered deeply into the history of salvation, Mary, in a way, unites in her person and re-echoes the most important doctrines of the faith: and when she is the subject of preaching and worship she prompts the faithful to come to her Son, to his sacrifice and to the love of the Father. Seeking after the glory of Christ, the Church becomes more like her lofty type, and continually progresses in faith, hope and charity, seeking and doing the will of God in all things. The Church, therefore, in her apostolic work too, rightly looks to her who gave birth to Christ, who was thus conceived of the Holy Spirit and born of a virgin, in order that through the Church he could be born and increase in the hearts of the faithful. In her life the Virgin has been a model of that motherly love with which all who join in the Church's apostolic mission for the regeneration of mankind should be animated.

IV. *The Cult of the Blessed Virgin*
in the Church

66. Mary has by grace been exalted above all angels and men to a place second only to her Son, as the most holy mother of God who was involved in the mysteries of Christ: she is rightly honored by a special cult in the Church. From the earliest times the Blessed Virgin is honored under the title of Mother of God, whose protection the faithful take refuge together in prayer in all their perils and needs.[21] Accordingly, following the Council of Ephesus, there was a remarkable growth in the cult of the People of God towards Mary, in veneration and love, in invocation and imitation, according to her own prophetic words: "all generations shall call me blessed, because he that is mighty hath done great things to me" (Lk. 1:48). This cult, as it has always existed in the Church, for all its uniqueness, differs essentially from the cult of adoration, which is offered equally to the Incarnate Word and to the Father and the Holy Spirit, and it is most favorable to it. The various forms of piety towards the Mother of God, which the Church has approved within the limits of sound and orthodox doctrine, according to the dispositions and understanding of the faithful, ensure that while the mother is honored, the Son through whom all things have their being (cf. Col.

21. *"Sub tuum praesidium."*

1:15–16) and in whom it has pleased the Father that all fullness should dwell (cf. Col. 1:19) is rightly known, loved and glorified and his commandments are observed.

67. The sacred synod teaches this Catholic doctrine advisedly and at the same time admonishes all the sons of the Church that the cult, especially the liturgical cult, of the Blessed Virgin, be generously fostered, and that the practices and exercises of devotion towards her, recommended by the teaching authority of the Church in the course of centuries be highly esteemed, and that those decrees, which were given in the early days regarding the cult images of Christ, the Blessed Virgin and the saints, be religiously observed.[22] But it strongly urges theologians and preachers of the word of God to be careful to refrain as much from all false exaggeration as from too summary an attitude in considering the special dignity of the Mother of God.[23] Following the study of Sacred Scripture, the Fathers, the doctors and liturgy of the Church, and under the guidance of the Church's magisterium, let them rightly illustrate the duties and privileges of the Blessed Virgin which always refer to Christ, the source of all truth, sanctity, and devotion. Let them carefully refrain from whatever might by word or deed lead the separated brethren or any others whatsoever into error about the true doctrine of the Church. Let the faithful remember moreover that true devotion consists neither in sterile or transitory affection, nor in a certain vain credulity, but proceeds from true faith, by which we are led to recognize the excellence of the Mother of God, and we are moved to a filial love towards our mother and to the imitation of her virtues.

V. *Mary, Sign of True Hope and Comfort*
for the Pilgrim People of God

68. In the meantime the Mother of Jesus in the glory which she possesses in body and soul in heaven is the image and beginning of the Church as it is to be perfected in the world to come. Likewise she shines forth on earth, until the day of the Lord shall come (cf. 2 Pet. 3:10), a sign of certain hope and comfort to the pilgrim People of God.

22. Council of Nicea II. A.D. 787: Mansi 13, 378–379; *Denz.* 302 (600–601). Council of Trent, Session 25: Mansi 33, 171–172.
23. Cf. Pius XII, radio message, 24 Oct. 1954: *AAS* 40 (1954), p. 670; Encycl. *Ad coeli Reginam*, 11 Oct. 1954. *AAS* 46 (1954), p. 637.

69. It gives great joy and comfort to this sacred synod that among the separated brethren too there are those who give due honor to the Mother of Our Lord and Saviour, especially among the Easterns, who with devout mind and fervent impulse give honor to the Mother of God, ever virgin.[24] The entire body of the faithful pours forth urgent supplications to the Mother of God and of men that she, who aided the beginnings of the Church by her prayers, may now, exalted as she is above all the angels and saints, intercede before her Son in the fellowship of all the saints, until all families of people, whether they are honored with the title of Christian or whether they still do not know the Saviour, may be happily gathered together in peace and harmony into one People of God, for the glory of the Most Holy and Undivided Trinity.

24. Cf. Pius XI, *Encycl. Ecclesiam Dei,* 12 Nov. 1923: AAS 15 (1923), p. 581; Pius XII, *Encycl. Fulgens corona,* 8 Sept. 1953: AAS 45 (1953), p. 590–591.

The Voice of the People of God

Sensus Fidelium

In the course of preparing to write this book I asked many of my friends: What would you like to find in a book about Mary? What should be said about Mary today? I would like to share here some excerpts from their responses, because I think these express what theologians call the *sensus fidelium*, the sense of the faithful, the deep understanding that rises among the people from living within the mystery of Christ in the Church today. This is the Mary that I have tried to present, however poorly, in the pages of this book.

*　*　*

I personally have deep feelings on the subject as our Lady is very close to me, never far from my thoughts.

I believe she has so much love to give each one of us that it is impossible to fathom. I see her as a mother who suffers for her children, is preoccupied with their wrongdoings and sorrows but never stops loving. I see her as happy, smiling, always ready to embrace, console, encourage. She is a mother in every sense of the word, seeking always for her children to be better. To go by the straight road—not to see any soul lost.

She wants to have us surrender to her Son totally and all her work on earth is to promote this, to make us better, holier people.

—*A young woman in high school*

*　*　*

I feel Mary's Jewish background is most important and her times in history, because of what it meant then, for example, to risk pregnancy without marriage (today a little voice from heaven would be charming   to try a mystical experience).

Is it that Mary so became one in her love for God that she

physically carried the Christ? I guess each of us carries Christ
—but many of us are not able to be a true *fiat.*

—A wife and mother

*   *   *

Contemporary women could be led into a more contemplative
life-style by being led to Mary as woman, wife, mother. Is she
an anachronism for us today? The clichés about her could be
explained; that is, the essence of femininity, devotion, gentle-
ness. We have all read this and heard of this since grammar
school, but is anyone really paying serious attention to it?

Today's woman is going against her Mary nature. And men
need to liberate their feminine side.

Why was she chosen? What qualities were hers to be able to
mother Jesus, to be a part of his life and development into
adulthood?

—A wife and mother

*   *   *

My family and I, we have a very special devotion to Mary. We
try to do a little extra. So I am happy to relay my thoughts to
you.

There are two aspects I think that I would love to hear about
her if I were reading a book at this time: it would be about the
Virgin of the Poor and also *Our Lady of the Loving Heart.* These two
topics, I feel, in today's world would be very meaningful to me.
I leave them in your thoughts.

—A business executive, father of a growing family

*   *   *

I would like to help you out with the topic of Mary, but I have
difficulty with my perception of Mary. I think any book about
Mary today should include her recent appearances. I would be
interested in another viewpoint, and I am sure others would
too. I believe she appears at Medjugorje and suggest maybe
you go there before you begin writing. I think you should
include a discussion of the treatment of Mary by other Christian religions.

—President of a catholic foundation, wife and mother

* * *

What would you dwell on? Her beauty, her love, her rosary; how saints and sinners alike become eternally in love with her; the list is infinite.

—A father

* * *

I have long felt that the sexual revolution and women's lib are based on a faulty theology related to Manichaeism, i.e., in so far as they are objectionable. Of course, there are some very good insights into aspects of both areas that are based on the best of our Catholic tradition. But I believe that one of the major contributions to marian studies today would be to work out, at some depth and detail, a solid theological basis as to what is positive in feminine sexuality and indicate its complementary role to the masculine—and vice versa for Christology and for masculine spirituality. It may be premature to attempt such a study in a book on Mary before adequate monographs have been done. But in a book on Mary today I would think that a serious effort along these lines would prove to be a most pertinent contribution today.

—A Cistercian abbot

* * *

What I would like to find in such a book would be a reflection on the attitude of Mary during the different incidents presented in the Gospels where she is mentioned, with an application (very discreet but effective) to our lives: Mary's spirit of faith, abandonment, confidence, self-denial, prayer, love, etc. I believe at the moment people want more something that begins from Scripture rather than from theology. But we should not forget the more supernatural aspects of Mary's vocation: daughter of God the Father, mother of Christ, spouse of the Holy Spirit. This is also important for us, for what shows forth the marvelous works of God invites us to thanksgiving and wonder (very important for the life of prayer) as well as an attitude of confidence.

—A Belgian abbess

* * *

On reading your letter the first thought that came to my mind was Mary's centering—Mary beckons us to the center.

Mary was making a center for the Lord, the Son of God could not resist her prayer of submission, abandonment, letting go of her possibility to be mother of the Messiah. He, the Christ, was the enfleshed center in Mary.

At the visitation, forgetting herself completely, she leaps to her sister Elizabeth, leaving even dwelling on her tremendous privilege—unaware of all but helping the aged Elizabeth. She brings the Center to her cousin, the Voice and the Eternal Word engage in a dance at the center of both hallowed wombs.

Nativity—Mary beckons the shepherds to approach the Center—no need for words, but for adoration and contemplation.

Presentation—Mary brings the Center to Simeon and Anna.

Finding Jesus at the Center. Uncertain at first, he tells her he was at the Center with the Father.

Mary's many visitations to this world, always beckoning us to the Center—her role in this—the prayer word, be it mantra, one of the ninety-nine names of Allah, etc.—Mary beckons, Lourdes, Fátima, Knock, etc.

My response:

Be with us, Mary, along the way, at every step we take, lead us to Jesus your loving Son. Come with us, Mary, come.

—A missionary sister

❖ ✱ ✱

I have been thinking quite a bit about your recent request for what I think about Mary.

Sometimes my husband tells me I've been in the mountains too long and that I've forgotten there's a big world out there. In the mountains, Mary may creep into people's consciousness a wee bit at Christmas, along with the stable, shepherds and star. But she's a nonentity here.

As a child and as a young woman, I guess I had a romanticized impression of her with all the sweetness and pietistic notions possible, and she was a distant, frankly unattainable idea that one believed in. Practically all the titles attributed to her in her litany, while being beautifully poetic and of Biblical and traditional origin, somehow made her more unreal. So for years I struggled with the concept of Mary, and that basically is what she was for me—a concept, not a real person. She was a fleeting figure in the gospels and most of the Marianistic devotions infuriated me because they seemed to reinforce all those pietistic notions, and I sensed something was wrong. Sure, I read about her and her great "fiat," prayed the rosary, even listened to tapes about her, but still something was lacking.

It wasn't until a year or two ago that she came to life for me. I remember the event quite clearly. I had taken Marilyn T. to the utility company in Pinesville to help her get "juice" (electricity) turned on. Marilyn, her husband and her baby had been living in a shed out in a hollow, and now finally her husband had found some little job which would enable them to move into a shack and have electricity. While waiting for the lady at the desk, I sat looking at Marilyn—young, gaunt, listless, long stringy hair, dirty clothes and feet, holding her child to her in an exhausted manner, and the only thought which came to me was of the Madonna and Child.

From that point on, Mary began to take on life for me as a person. She had been homeless, had her baby in a hovel with no clothes or heat, was lucky to have the water available for the animals, all this to satisfy the red tape of authorities. Can you picture a pregnant woman who is due to deliver her baby riding a donkey? Was it better or worse than a rickety truck on a mountain-hollow unpaved road. Physical poverty is real, and it is ugly and dirty.

Can you imagine her fear and horror at the slaughter? She and her family fled the same way other families are forced to flee today to avoid being massacred. They didn't cross the desert into Egypt in an air-conditioned Land Rover and arrive there fresh and clean and welcomed. They were dispossessed, refugees. Strangers in a strange land, the same as so many who leave their homes to seek survival elsewhere—whether it's an Appalachian family leaving their mountains to seek employment in the cities or a Haitian in the United States or a Central American in a neighboring country.

She lost her child for a few days, but wasn't she fortunate to find him in a temple? So many mothers today find theirs on the streets of large cities.

I guess what I'm trying to say is that Mary is our hope and

advocate because she's been there. She has endured the sufferings of humanity, sufferings which women especially endure to this day: poverty, rejection, dispossession, loss. The artist or intellectual in us delights in all the exquisite attributes of Mary, so rightfully hers as Mother of God, Mother of God who assumed humanity. If her heart was indeed pierced by the sword, then surely her immaculate conception did not make her immune to pain and suffering.

So many artists, books, etc. are written for the elite of Christianity, but I truly wish the poor could speak to them and transmit a bit of reality to them. Recently, I listened to tapes on Mary by a woman theologian, and while some sections were enlightening and informative, the whole left me unsatisfied, again with that sense of unreality, that sense of Mary as a concept or abstraction rather than a person.

It may be that I am so surrounded by suffering and trauma and have experienced my own fair share of it that I'm simply projecting a need for hope, for someone whose personal experience has been similar to understand and say, "It's all right. My Son will take care of it. Don't despair. He and I have been through this and we know the pain." That's why the "Salve" has usually been my prayer to Mary. "To you do we cry—to you do we send up our sighs, mourning and weeping in this valley of tears."

While at Knock this summer, I had a moment with Mary. I wept as I had needed to weep for many, many years as I shared the pain of seeing my son suffer. She had seen her Son suffer, and I knew she understood and the floodgates opened.

Incidentally, isn't it interesting that so many apparitions of Mary were to children, poor illiterate children and peasants? I think it is from the poor that we can learn to know Mary. Even if they don't know her, their very lives can teach us.

Maybe my husband is right. I've been in the mountains too long and I'm out of touch with mainstream Catholic America. Regardless, I would say that if I can have one request, let it be that you write about Mary's humanity, treat her as a person and hear what the poor say about her.

—*A woman in Appalachian ministry*

* * *

I've become your "researcher" and have asked the following people what they would like to have included in the book about Mary:

1. Our Centering Prayer Director: Saturate us with her life, especially the feast days. We need to have so much more written about her.

2. A Sister who counsels the divorced and separated: her humanity; even though she was fearful, her acceptance and trust.

3. Director of Religious Education: her feelings as a mother, how she felt when he left as a boy and at his death.

4. A widow in our Centering Prayer group: Mary as a mother to her family.

5. A woman in my lay ministry class: Mary's intercessory prayer, why Mary has communicated specifically with children and teenagers.

6. Lay Minister: More about Mary's trust and fears.

7. Director of Lay Ministry: Mary's discipleship.

8. Myself: Mary's humility in being chosen Jesus' mother, accepting God's will with complete faith and affirmation. Mary's visiting Elizabeth was so human, to seek company (and perhaps comfort) at the most beautiful time of her life.

—An elderly lay woman

* * *

You mentioned your future book on Mary. I immediately thought of the many and varied books on the subject. There are so many that portrayed her in a plaster cast, and some that gushed with inane devotion, and some that made her look like a veritable goddess! Do bring her down to earth with all her beautiful traits. I like to see Mary as a down-to-earth person, a woman of worth, attainable as a model. I bought a statue of Mary for a friend in the restaurant business. It shows her as a young woman with an apron and rather drab clothes, as befits someone working in the kitchen. On her head a sort of caplike bandanna. In her hand she holds a broom to sweep. She is in a position for work. This human Mary is depicted as ready or already working. This type of Mary is seldom represented in literature. I like to see this old-fashioned young woman as she develops in life as part of the human race. Does the fact that she was sinless deny that she must have had the same human qualities as other women, not only of her time and culture, but also suitable for today's time and culture? The basics are rather stable in a changing world. At times it seems as if her Son Jesus is more human and earthy than she is supposed to be. The theological Mary served her purpose when I was a seminarian and studying mariology was appropriate. Now what is needed is an appreciation of her true value as a beautiful person, an emerging woman on her way to fulfill her destiny which involved all humankind in a timeless and eternal dimension. The first fruits of the Son's resurrection should not be an abstract ideal of humanity that will be read like mythological fiction, devoid of anything truly human. That is why I think we need Mary to be our companion and guide as a human person and a truly feeling and emotional woman whom we can approach on our own level.

—A religious priest

* * *

I think we grew up with a concept of Mary that was unreal. It was an overly pious approach that made Mary unattainable. I got the idea that it was almost impossible to approach God, so we "went to Mary." It was as if Mary was a quasi-divine "beggar" of gifts and graces from Jesus, whose hurt and anger at us could only be appeased by her. Granted, this is a caricature from childhood, a hurtful one.

We also got in the "theological race" to see who could be remembered for honoring Mary in the Church of our day— Mediatrix of Graces, the definition of the Assumption, etc. Finally, there were the "private revelations"—Lourdes, Fatima, et al. I am not saying that these have no value, but they often became the source of superstition or fanaticism.

At some point I put Mary on a shelf to be admired—and avoided. Even our Mariology courses in the seminary only reinforced my suspicions. The turning point for me was the letter of Pope Paul VI on devotion to Mary. I finally met the Mary of Scripture and found her to be alive and well. The door opened when I was able to see Mary as a disciple. It was the beginning of my rediscovery of her and renewed devotion. I began to see her as a role model for today's woman, and a model for authentic liberation—all of this began to make sense.

I still become angry when Paul VI's work is ignored (most people have never heard of it) and we return to such things as the Blue Army and other such devotional groups. While there is some good in these, there is a lot of bad theology, and unhealthy pre–Vatican II conservatism.

The Mary I love is:

> Mother of the Church and our mother
> first and finest disciple
> hearing the word and sharing the mission of Jesus
> sensitive to the poor and oppressed
> obedient and humble in responding to the everyday
> situations of life

The more traditional theological conclusions are valid to be sure but they need to be reinterpreted and presented today so as to help, not hinder, our understanding of the real Mary.

—A parish priest

* * *

Writing on Mary today, describe the new marian sanctuaries and the vast pilgrimages to them—the first is Medjugorje in Yugoslavia . . . Athos is, of course, a fief of Our Lady. You were there. In the Soviet Union there are many marian centers.

Write on Peace. Our Lady is Queen of peace and of the nations, Mother of all Christians.

—An Orthodox layman

* * *

You ask "what you would want to find in a book on Mary today." My spontaneous answer would certainly be: I would like to learn, if possible, about the origins of the great Cistercian devotion to our Lady. . . .

If you care to discuss the problem of Mark's exclusion of the Mother of Jesus from discipleship . . .

I find it interesting that our Lady was already in the first Christian century a "bone of contention." I once ventured the opinion that the title, "the Mother of the Lord" is an indication (at least in the Lucan church) of very early devotion to Mary. . . .

* * *

What would I like to find in a book about Mary?

a. Mary seems to be forgotten today in a world which seeks good *role models*. Maybe the world needs to rediscover her *relevance*.

b. How does Mary fit in with regard to *other states of life* aside from the married state? The religious, the single, the divorced, etc., might find new strength in getting to know her better as well as married couples, where her role as mother might seem more identifying. Maybe it is the modern media which is emphasizing accepting Christ but sort of forgetting all the rich tradition which might lead one to come to such a decision and live it faithfully.

c. Our world is complex today. . . . She was simple and open. Where can we *bridge the gap here?* Again, her relevance to us today.

d. Finally, we face problems like nuclear war, the deadly AIDS epidemic, unwanted pregnancies, injustice—how can rediscovering the personhood of Mary deliver our world from modern-day sufferings and *lead us* to the love of the Father? Why do we not respond to God as she *naturally* did?

—*A middle-age layman*

* * *

I would like to see a book that isn't full of pious stuff. We now live in an era that is not too concerned with Mary (at least my generation). The world is not concerned with virginity or blue as a color that is to be inspiring or moving as perhaps it once was or is for senior Christians with a good amount of pious upbringing.

Who is she to the post-Christian era? I am not so sure it would be easy to answer this question. The rosary is misunderstood. To some extent it seems like a voodoo practice: say some Hail Marys and everything will be O.K. As for myself I believe I understand.

I would hate to see another book that will be put up on nice catholic people's bookshelves who will say isn't that nice. As for myself I struggle that there is too much talk about and not enough being to the Father.

—A young airplane steward

* * *

Back to Mary! She has been and still is a major force in my spiritual life. She took me to Jesus (in the Catholic Church) during college days and then to the convent. I would never have lasted through those desert years without her presence and warmth and strength and compassion. Through her I saw the feminine side of God that has been so neglected in our Western fall/redemption, patriarchal, male-dominated, left-brain spirituality. *I would like to see a book underlining Mary as the greatest expression of creation spirituality.*

Her spirit is not a back door to heaven for catholics, but the front door into the kingdom of heaven present here and now for us to live in, rejoice in, grow in. Jesus came proclaiming, The kingdom of God is at hand. He is still telling us: Wake up! Look! God provides at every moment in your life everything that you need to be fully alive and happy *now*. We are growing in more awareness every day, expanding always to other horizons; death is simply a final expansion with no limit but God.

To me then, faith as trust is the key and Mary lived this totally and gives us this key. We have to use it every day. We trust God's gifts and grace in every situation. Or don't we? Our awareness and growth depend on our willingness to trust his love, it seems to me. What did Elizabeth say to Mary? "Blessed is she who has trusted in the Lord's word." We go from blessing to blessing as the Truth of Life and Mary helps us to see and experience that Truth.

—A woman in campus ministry

* * *

It was only on the day of his death and by means of a TV news broadcast that a mother learned that her priest son actually died of AIDS. The whole family withdrew into shocked isolation. Can such mothers learn something from Mary who at the

Cross accepted John as her own son? May Mary be their consolation and strength.

—A gay priest

*   *   *

It is hard to say what I would like to see written about Mary,
particularly now when I can hardly see through another bout
of loneliness. The navy . . . this place is a desert. Mary! Tell
us what she has for people who are bound now in America by
freedom. Tell us if there is any way that we can get back in
touch. Undoubtedly you will mention centering somewhere. I
am aware of your vision of the individual beauty that God has
bestowed upon us. I am truncated, my whole expansion frus-
trated—quite a few times by my own ignorance or the force of
circumstances. Mary? Hail Mary, full of grace . . . Jesus . . .
now and at the hour of our death. Amen. How sacred is the
womb. How far from the sacred intuition of women are men.

—A young sailor